RETURN FROM ENLIGHTENMENT

FOREST K. DAVIS

ADAMANT PRESS
Adamant, Vermont
1971

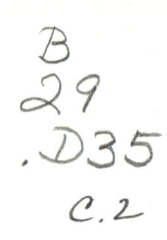

Copyright © 1971 by Forest K. Davis

International Standard Book Number   0-912362-01-4 (Clothbound)
International Standard Book Number   0-912362-02-2 (Paperbound)

Library of Congress Card Catalogue Number   74-155656

First Edition

Printed at the Pine Hill Printery, Freeman, South Dakota 57029

Distributed by the Adamant Press, Box 7, Adamant, Vermont, 05640

To Dr. and Mrs. Rembert Stokes
Wilberforce, Ohio
- with honor and affection
- SKA
November 1971

Other Publications

Toward a Revised Philosophy of the Paper Machine. Des Plaines, Illinois, *Paper Industry* Magazine, 1964.

Editor, Slylvia Bliss, *Quests.* Montpelier, Vermont. Capital City Press, 1965.

Inscription

Alice Lake Herriott

September 29th, 1892　　　　　　January 25th, 1964
Winfield, Kansas　　　　　　　　　Calais, Vermont

Inheritor of strong traditions of New England and the central states; forthright as her Kansas countrymen. A teacher of biology and general science for twenty-eight years in the great public high schools of Upper Manhattan and the Bronx; her homes standing open to visitors from many lands, her habits of warmth and welcome becoming the standards of her peers, arts and ideas flowing freely around her. Builder of patterns in the midst of life, her enduring monument the happier ways of men. A spirit glowing, for whom life's end was affirmation.

> "Earth has not anything to show more fair:
> Dull would he be of soul who could pass by
> A sight so touching in its majesty:
> This city now doth like a garment wear
> The beauty of the morning; silent, bare,
> Ships, towers, domes, theatres, and temples lie
> Open unto the fields, and to the sky;
> All bright and glittering in the smokeless air.
> Never did sun more beautifully steep
> In his first splendour valley, rock, or hill;
> Never saw I, never felt, a calm so deep!
> The river glideth at his own sweet will:
> Dear God! the very houses seem asleep;
> And all that mighty heart is lying still!"
>
> —Wordsworth
> "... Westminster Bridge"
> 1803

Appreciations

Grateful acknowledgment is made to the following journals which have courteously granted permission to revise and reprint papers originally appearing in their pages:

to *Crozer Quarterly,* since replaced by the *Crozer Voice,* of Crozer Theological Seminary, Chester, Pennsylvania, for "Communism As Religion" from Vol. XXVIII, No. 3, July 1951;

to *The Antioch Review* of Yellow Springs, Ohio, for "Education Is One" from the Fall 1955 issue;

to the *Journal of Higher Education,* Ohio State University Press, Columbus, Ohio, for "Conjunction Over Harvard" from Vol. XXX, No. 5, May 1959;

to the Unitarian Universalist *Register-Leader,* of Boston, Mass., for "Kierkegaard's Judgment: The Attack Upon Christendom" from Vol. CXXXVIII, No. 10, December 1959;

to *Educational Theory,* of the University of Illinois at Urbana, Illinois, for "The Philosophy Of Knowledge" from Vol. VIII, No. 4, October 1958, and "World-View As Ground Of Morality" from Vol. XI, No. 3, July 1961;

to the *Crane Review,* of Crane Theological School (since discontinued), Tufts University, Medford, Mass., for "The Invisible Man Re-born" from Vol. II, No. 1, Fall 1959; for "The Essential Identity Of Near-Contemporary Cultural Movements" from Vol. III, No. 2, Winter 1961; and for "The Chariot-Wheels Of King Milinda" from Vol. V, Nos. 2-3, Winter-Spring 1963;

to the *Midwest Quarterly,* of Kansas State College, Pittsburg, Kansas, for "Existentialisms As Interstices" from Vol. XII, No. 1, Oct. 1970;

and to *The Yale Review,* of New Haven, Connecticut, for "American Education As Metaphysics: The Religious Consequence", from Vol. LXI, No. 1, Autumn 1971.

The editors have enabled revisions due to the passage of time so that the papers may appear here in slightly altered form. Footnotes have been omitted or incorporated in the text. Alterations in content have tended to be matters of perspective or style.

The papers included in this collection have for the most part derived rather simply and directly from one or another stage of personal and professional experience. The eleventh and twelfth were originally among working-papers prepared for a Vermont Program in Non-Western Studies, a Ford Foundation undertaking for faculty delegates from Vermont colleges and universities. The purpose of these informal discussions was to broaden the education of college teachers who were not specialists in Eastern or other regional studies but who wished to take further account of Eastern, African, and other non-Western cultures in their teaching. The seminars invited a variety of cultural specialists from out-of-state institutions to present materials from time to time. Seminar members were free to follow their own interests in constructing report-papers. The Program has courteously granted the use of the two report-papers included here, but it is of course not accountable for any irresponsible notions which may be contained in them. Professor Herbert McArthur, then of the University of Vermont and librarian of the Program, was especially helpful with bibliographical suggestions and with original ideas from his own writings.

In making a primary statement of position, whatever the reservations that may apply to it, inevitably one's mind turns to the materials from which one's foundations have been constructed. It is difficult to know whether to speak of one's teachers of a generation and more ago, answering the sense of honor and obligation, or to keep silent, leaving their retirements and their memories in peace, unentangled in possible controversy for which they bear not the slightest responsibility. In a period marked from time to time by waves of criticism of American public high schools it is only just to remember how many great teachers have served and serve today in these remarkable educational institutions. The high school graduate must often carry into later life enormous indebtedness to the teachers of earlier years. To take but the present instance, to Doris S. Barnes, Martha C. Cramer, Elizabeth F. Cornell, Marion E. Lord, and Edmund Keefe, all of Nashua, N. H. Senior High School, and to Anna P. Butler, Margaret Ford, Adele Schroeder, Eva M. Ruggli, and Ethel V.

Sampson, all of Cambridge, Mass. High and Latin School, the recollections of former students must constantly return in profound appreciation.

Harvard is always staffed with the titans of an age. The memories of a single student can only begin the roll of the great teachers of his undergraduate and graduate years: James Buell Munn, William Ernest Hocking, George Shannon Forbes, Gregory P. Baxter, John Tucker Murray, Willard Llearoyd Sperry, Julius Seelye Bixler, Robert H. Pfeiffer, Henry Joel Cadbury. It may be as well that teachers do not know how often and with what appreciation their students remember them; the entailments might be greater than they should bear.

From colleagues of recent years at Goddard College in Vermont and Wilberforce University in Ohio have come uncounted moments of rewarding challenge and reflection. In clearest mercy these persons are omitted here. Many would hold different views of topics under discussion; they should be free of burdens in these pages. Let them be warned, however; such restraint will not endure forever. Goddard and Wilberforce alike present, each in its own distinctive way, too interesting and too significant a brace of histories for them not to be fully told; in the course of time there are those who will surely recount them in one way or another.

Every teacher has the heaviest of obligations to his students. At Goddard where everyone feels firmly in the forefront of almost everything one of the strongest commitments of a student is likely to be to the re-education of his teachers. In keenness of mind and awareness of issues, in verbal capacity and audacity, in plain persistence, in determined examination of questions, the Goddard student is simply outstanding; and if his teachers should not also stand out in the taking of gaff there are fortunately other colleges and universities where they can go to rest and recover their equilibrium. Goddard students have combined their considerable forces to assist in creating one of the unusual college communities of our time, and it should be added, they have done so with memorable kindness of heart. Few teachers with experience in that singular community do not know the degree to which their heightening lives of thought and study have depended on the insatiable, friendly, often brilliant students who in a manner of speaking would as soon box their ears as listen to anything they say.

At Wilberforce, long an institutional leader in the higher education of predominantly Black young people, a different but equally significant contribution is being made to American higher education. Several years must elapse for such a broad and deep period of learning to ripen to the point of commentary. To this irreplaceable educational experience one will hope to return in later collections of essays.

Of particular persons to whom appreciation repairs in strong measure, these individuals stand among many: Alexander Tarwater of Nashua, N. H., a tuner of pianos who taught informally the disciplines of large and little things, as well as a fundamental trust in nature; Martha Moriarty of the Nashua elementary schools, and Edna P. Hoitt, Agnes E. Shea and Thomas Hargroves of the Nashua Junior High School; Elizabeth Spring of the Nashua Public Library; Katharine Kendall Bartlett of Baltimore, of most courteous recollection; Elizabeth Kent Gay of Calais, Vermont and Hanover, N. H., for trenchant expression of general ideas on occasions which she may not remember; Frank Wilbur Herriott of Union Theological Seminary, New York and Brook House, Calais, Vermont, for depth of understanding and a lifetime of thoughtfulness; Alfred Pol Nicholas Stiernotte of Quinnipiac College, Hamden, Connecticut, for bibliographical suggestions and for his ranging insights; Alexander Elliott Peaston, Minister of the Non-Subscribing Presbyterian Church of Dromore, County Down, scholar in the English tradition, friend in a universal tradition; Arthur Wright Chickering of East Montpelier, Vermont and Washington, D. C., scholar in the American tradition, a thoughtful and tolerant listener, full of ideas and of challenge, whose cool pond and warm view have informed many a conversation; and at long last, the magnificent Frederick May Eliot of Boston, longtime head of the American Unitarian Association, a forceful and towering figure who broods today over every conference table in the liberal church, his splendor undimmed by the passing of years.

In the pages to follow it will appear that certain pivotal intellectual obligations of a less personal but equally powerful nature are also owed. The text will be clear on these several points and persons; one does not in any wise forget them.

Among all of these not a single one bears the slightest responsibility for what is said here, but each has given of his genius in special ways: to each may the waters return a thousandfold.

Foreword: Recurrent Themes

It could be argued that every reflective person expresses in the patterns of his thought a number of recurrent themes, major for him, major or minor in the larger context, which emerge persistently, repeating themselves so to speak accidentally, from his personal history, experience, and prime intellectual involvements. Typically, there may be little he can do to change these involuntary emphases. They are the forms in accordance with which he constructs intelligibility. They constitute his assumptions on the nature of things. They and the relationships between them comprise his logic. Logics are peculiar. The natural orders of one mind may not be those of another. It may be only the occasional logic which becomes abstract and general enough to be taught as a subject in a classroom.

The papers presented in this book, dating from the mid-1950's to the mid-1960's, illustrate the point. At times diverse of origin, they resolve around a few pervasive themes inadvertently surfacing in the welter of observations and experiences which no human life can escape.

Operational thought, referring to the characteristic by which an expressional mode defines itself, is one such principal theme. It is related to the problem of systematics, an unfashionable concern in a pluralistic age, yet a stubborn fascination of mind involved in ideas. What happens when partial systems, limited ranges of awareness, are encouraged in self-definition, in serving as grounds for systematic extension and expansion? What gets done as a result, and is therefore useful? What is hindered or obscured, and is therefore of less value if not of actual disvalue?

Implications of behaviors and patterns of thought make up another theme. Perhaps there may be an identifiable ecology of thought, as when a woodland environment passes through set stages the plant growths of which can be predicted between one hardwood cover and the next. Will we someday be able to calculate when the next rationalist or naturalist school will appear?

Among the acute needs of our time is a philosophy of conflict, still another principal theme. The nature of conflict conceived of as configuration of communication and dependency, indeed as a relationship of commonality rather than of simple opposition, will bear study far beyond these pages. The masques and forms of ideas backwards and forwards in time as well as across chasms of the present day are involved in this focus of concern,—that which seems to be one thing, and which may in one setting even be that one thing, which in a different setting may instead—or also—be another thing. What would be the reality of an apparent opposition in social or political philosophy if it should appear that elements in conflict consistently held large areas in common?—that some parts of the configurations bore notable resemblances to other parts?—that a particular conflict might be a habit or desire, a form of needed communication like diplomacy or conversation or the simple exchange of literatures and cultural expressions? What implications for social or political policy might follow?

Education as a dimension of the real, as a vehicle and form of life and thought, is yet another recurrent theme. Education is a way of life in America, pervasive of business and industry, of art, agriculture, technology, what one will; by no means limited to schools and institutions, it comes and goes with the movements and concerns of persons. Should it not be recognized as social metaphysics, an expressional form and activity in which can be cast the very nature of social and intellectual process, at least on this peculiar continent? Are the realities of one continent so very different from the realities of other continents, those drifting platelets of the earth's crust?

Finally, but far from last in a context of reflective themes, is that of knowing in relation to the real, an intensely metaphysical articulation of subject and object the polarities of which are still, after centuries of effort, open to re-definition and new modes of understanding. Are not movement and relation among elements and components of the real defined by ways of knowing? And are not the ways of knowing defined also by what there is to be known? Is this apparent circularity an obscuring or a clarifying characteristic? Does it mean that awareness is a balance of subjective and objective factors, neither category of which can be considered apart from the other, and that the weights of traditional epistemologies in one direction or the other have now to be loosened and left to find their temporary points of rest? If this should occur, what would be the consequences for the settled philosophic stances of today or times past?

Among these interwoven themes will be found most of the concerns of the papers which follow. As with any initiative in discussion, they are intended to encourage dialogue, not to end it. If in places a conclusive conviction reveals itself, the history of thought has after all been constructed of just such slips of tongue or mind. It is no great matter. The waves of tides incoming will soon reduce the fortress. Even now the formulations of future days can be anticipated, welcomed as the play of children or the wisdom of philosophers, watched and cared for in their preoccupations, earnestly working at the castles of tomorrow.

—Yellow Springs, Ohio
November 7th, 1970

Table of Contents

	Appreciations	v
	Foreword: Recurrent Themes	ix
I	The Invisible Man Re-born	1
II	The Philosophy of Knowledge	15
III	Kierkegaard's Judgment: The Attack Upon Christendom	24
IV	Existentialisms As Interstices	32
V	Education Is One	41
VI	Conjunction Over Harvard: Religion and the University Form a New Configuration	50
VII	American Education As Metaphysics: The Religious Consequence	55
VIII	The Essential Identity of Near-Contemporary Cultural Movements	66
IX	World-View As Ground of Morality: A Phase of the Metaphysics of Education	79
X	Communism As Religion	90
XI	Apparent Religious Themes in Contemporary Mainland China	101
XII	The Chariot-Wheels of King Milinda	117
XIII	The Arrow and the Song: A Note on the Metaphysics of History	134
XIV	Return From Enlightenment	139
	Bibliographic Notes	145
	Index	151

I The Invisible Man Re-Born

The compelling characteristics of the studies of man have understandably challenged much of the intelligence which recent times could bring to bear on questions of ultimate meaning. In some form this has always been so, for Shakespeare and Socrates were also students of their peers. Problems of personality and the relations of men have provided points of fascination since the earliest hours of human consciousness. But the studies recorded through literature and the arts have been essentially poetic in kind, in that they have derived from the natural interests men have had in the situations of other men, and in that the methods and materials used have been those of the creative mind attending to a problem with the lay resources at hand. The judgments and descriptions resulting have often been among the noblest of cultural achievements. It is as if the contemplation of life were a major objective of the existence of life, and as if artistic descriptions of human nature were the chief modes of expression in this region of fundamental interest. Whether this remains the case in a highly organized and professionalized period is part of the matter to be considered.

In short, mankind has enjoyed being able to gaze at itself around corners, with its eye, so to speak, on a stalk; and, not infrequently taking the part for whole, men have perceived now and then some significant fragment or aspect which has been assumed to represent all of personality. The genius and the danger of many kinds of study are comprised in this process; the aspect is real and can be described by whatever method is most useful, but the aspect is not the whole. If in the social sciences of the 20th century a strain of investigative genius has been codified, let it be remembered that the peril of generalized minuteness may have been codified with it.

In the non-systematic, individually creative dimensions of study, the succession of thoughtful insights and artistic descriptions have tended to balance each other. Each stage of judgment concerning the nature of things is inevitably followed by variant positions, for the need which men have to construct pictures of themselves remains insatiable, and the assumptions involved in a variety of positions are as divergent as the concerns and circumstances of origin. Knowledge until modern times has been mainly artistic or poetic in quality, individually conceived and confirmed, individually expressed in literature, the fine arts, even in occasional reflective systems of thought; and, in the end, individually appreciated, for part of the function of the arts in any form is to serve the creating artist, and part is to serve the appreciating observer. The contemplation of life has lately been professionalized, however. The arts have given way to the social sciences. In place of *Oedipus Rex* there is now the Oedipus complex.

This may or may not be a useful development. Insights do derive from properties of large aggregates. Personality can be partially described in terms of social relations, and in fact this is of immense value, for social investigation discovers unfamiliar facets of human nature and establishes the significance of relatedness for the individual and the group. Still the question arises whether the hooks of personality ought to be the chief material from which a conception of man is to be drawn. Informative as relationships may be, uncritical dependence upon the social husks selected by particular methods of study produces the onion theory of personality, in accordance with which the integumental layers are regarded as the substance as well as the attributes of human nature.

Some may feel that conceptions of the nature of man have no major role in the pattern of individual lives, or that they are not even regularly built by the mind out of materials at its disposal. But this approach is surely as absurd as ideas are likely to get in a time when subjectivists, positivists, beatniks, and existentialists are elbowing the dignified shades of the older idealisms in a succession of efforts to illumine new facades of man's nature. There is an obvious social utility to most of it, albeit also a considerable cost in the waste of energy and life, and much of it is cut from the same cloth. The nature of man himself appears to be an implicit if not explicit conceptual element in effective views of the world, and even in obscure systems can usually be uncovered if proper questions are addressed to the patterns of conduct which express them. It seems fair to hold a principle responsible for the active policy which exemplifies it, and an active policy responsible for the principle which it represents, whether or not they acknowledge each other.

The social sciences are ways of looking for what can be perceived about people, patterns of behavior and measurable characteristics, and it is from these social aspects of human nature that many of the ready-to-wear versions of it are frequently constructed. It ought to be possible to reverse the process and peel the aspects, discovering the substance. But when this is done there tends to be in current interpretations nothing left but a pile of shavings on the floor. One is reminded of the old film of "The Invisible Man," H. G. Wells' tale of a clever person who had a drug which allowed him to be invisible as long as he did not upset the furniture or otherwise give notice of his presence. The only trouble was that the drug slowly affected his mind. As the film opens a solitary figure enters swathed in heavy garments; his bandaged head reveals the outlines of a face. With ominous glee he takes off his hat and coat and gloves and begins to unwrap his head; but within the glove there is no hand and within the cloth no head or face; the thing becomes inhuman; garments fall away as in a frenzy until there is only a headless, vacant shirt dancing and capering insanely before a mirror. This too is tumbled off; the room seems weirdly empty; a door jumps open, footsteps fade away, and backward floats the laughter of a madman.

So re-appears one of the oldest of questions: What is the reality behind the aspects? If the aspects are peeled away, is nothing left? Can husks enclose a cipher? Do successive layers of process comprise an object? This type of query seems very much alive in the common regions of physics and philosophy, so that it may be helpful to consider some of the implications of the operational approach. For present purposes the interest will be in the implications of operationalism for a conception of human nature rather than for the works of physics. It appears that there is more than a small implication here of individual man at work in significant ways, even though the universe in which he works is enormously enlarged to his awareness.

Operational Modes of Thought

In natural and social investigation as in systematic contemplation generally, the order of effort is common. In some way it seems fundamental that to resolve a problem the questioner must pose an answer and then look to see if the supposition was right. The mind supplies a solution or a series of possible solutions; through confirmatory tests the proposal will be established, selected, or denied. There are various ways of describing the operations of the mind within this interpretation. The general approach is a conceptualist one in that significant mental activity, of which knowledge is a part, is defined as an active motion of the mind which prehends objects and establishes relations, and by making use of patterns is able to produce at least tentative solutions to problems in the factual world by making use of the world of ideas. The ascription of reality to ideas and the mind, and the recognition of the initiatives of mind, contribute to the definition of the individual as an independent entity and responsible motivating force, capable of choice and decision.

Professor Bridgman has described this type of process in a particular way in his definition of operational method in theoretical physics. He felt that many conceptualizations are meaningless because the evidence for them cannot be checked in the way that evidence for scientifically useful concepts can be checked. His modification of intellectual process was to rule out of account questions and answers not derived from repeatable physical operations, and to define usable concepts in terms of the operations from which they were precipitated. He also enlarged upon the difficulty—indeed, the impossibility—of removing the observer from participation in the process which he is observing: even the supposedly objective scientist is very much in the midst of his experiments. That this is so is perhaps a simple recognition of the nature of science and of its close relation to other expressions of awareness.

The formulation of concepts remains a separate step in operational thought. Operationalism is an effort to tie a concept closely to the investigative procedure which produces or confirms it. Admissible evidence is that which lends itself to physical handling, as the definition of the field and the criterion of repeatability require. Bridgman provides, however, for conceptualizations of radically different and unexpected kinds based upon evidence not yet recognized and possibly not now acceptable.

It is an old game in philosophy to simplify the field of consideration by defining the evidence to be admitted, and then to broaden the definition to include almost the entire realm of human interest. The effect is to pick a point of reference as desired and to shift rather slightly the extension of reality being considered. Idea systems do this more or less regularly. Indeed, they could not otherwise hope to survive, since the tendency of the mind as traveller is to look out of the window to see what landmarks are in sight. A startling apparition can occasionally be accepted, as when on the train journey from Tokyo to Kamakura the Goddess of Mercy looms suddenly above the railyards of Ofuna. But for the most part the familiar reaches of experience had better be accounted for in the system or the philosopher could well save himself the labor of constructing it; the traveller will abandon so deceptive a means of travel and will very likely endanger the stability of things by going into philosophy for himself and undertaking to reconstruct the scenery.

As the content of a philosophic system must approximate the content of other systems, the distinctive remainder of a world-view is perhaps its approach or point of origin. Bridgman's system may illustrate the matter. He restricts the evidence sharply in the beginning but provides for unpredictable types of evidence to come to be regarded and eventually treated as physical. Only physically derived evidence is to be admitted, and for the time being this category will be carefully defined in limited terms; in the future, however, the term "physical" may be quite differently understood and its contents quite differently handled. Quite properly, Bridgman allows for this possibility. It is intended to be simply a general comment on the working of reflective systems to say that while he shepherds undesirable sheep out of his fold at one gate he appears to whistle them in at another. It is the present viewpoint that Bridgman is making a useful application in science of a general condition and principle of mental life.

Notice what this means. The conceptual nature of knowing confirms the contention of operational method that the topics being known depend heavily on the contribution made by the knower to the process of knowing. Conceptualism asserts that the procedure of becoming aware of anything to a degree which could be called knowing involves an initial activity of mind, while operationalism asserts that no knowledge is possible and no definitions derivable from knowledge are possible without describing the role of the knower as part of the knowing and the known.

Until now it has not been convenient to attend very much to these aspects of knowing. As so often happens, the introduction of a new perspective affects the broad relationships in which a familiar topic is seen to exist. To consider an example, visual perception has been conceived of in two ways—in medieval times as an emanation from the eye which encompassed the object being seen (a conception which may hereafter bear reconsideration), and in recent times as the passive response of a relatively inert receptor to active physical stimulation from outside the individual. If the conceptual nature of knowing is a defensible interpretation then the nature of knowing in general ought to be describable in operational terms. This does indeed appear to be the case. Knowledge in the western sense could at any time have been described in operational terms, that is, in terms of the physical operations and instruments in use in particular instances of knowing. There was never any need to do this, since in the dimension of visual perception the only instrument available for a long time was the human eye and all awarenesses of a spatial sort were based upon it. Equipment and method were common, yet both were indispensable elements in the definitions of nature reached through their use. The invention of the telescope would perhaps have made a very slight modification in the conceptualization enabled by the eye alone. Only in very recent times have extensions in the range of physical studies suggested that the eye is but one tool among many for the understanding of spatial relations, and that visual perception may be no more than one among many dimensions of comprehension of approximately the same order of data.

Human understanding is remarkably slow to change. Man remains very much a creature of his moment; his partial insights match only the hesitant conceptions which his mind dares to advance in the instant of his individual lifetime, confirmed by compliant segments of an agreeable and responsive universe. It is as if the natural universe were unbelievably complex in a diversity of dimensions, lending itself freely to interpretations of many kinds and on many levels. Man, the insatiable theorist, rushes at the towering crags of nature with conceptual claws agape, striking and tearing with the talons of the mind, wrenching off bits of material the substance of which to assay, in the image of which to characterize the known world. Universality enough inheres in local situations so that many of his hypotheses have worked well enough for their times and places. Olympus brooded over ancient Athens, serving to reflect what could otherwise not have been understood; notably, life went forward in the city across the plain, helped for the moment by the pantheon on the mountain which moved to meet and fill its vacant places as world-views always do. Similarly the intricate physics of modern times keeps its distance from the daily round, and yet provides the reflecting surface which sustains the dominant themes of the age. Life goes on its endless way in many conceptual settings; who is to know what the truth is, and whether the myth of today tells more than the myth of yesterday? The gods of Olympus long ago retired to the halls of legend; so also will the cold and careless universe of the twentieth century, its aimless globes crawling with vermin, rolling in meaningless silence through black desolation: this too will pass away.

The Problem of Judgment

A conviction emerges that man has consistently underdescribed himself in the modern period, not because he was compelled to do so, but mostly because he has been preoccupied with other parts of the problem of knowledge. He has inadvertently given in to the difficulty of conceiving an entity in general terms when his attention was necessarily applied to particular phases of it. The social sciences have discovered much that is of great value about human nature, the uses of which for the improvement of life have only begun to be made clear. But if one were to construct a total theory of man's nature out of the materials of the social sciences alone the likeness is hardly recognizable; man becomes rather some kind of walking onion whose interesting wrappings readily lend themselves to segmented study, less readily to general synthesis.

Scientific method itself, if the operational approach is to be taken seriously, is very much in flux and subject to gradual redefinition. It is not necessary to think of science as under attack; rather, it is simply in process of self-discovery and redescription. It is no longer safe to consider the Newtonian universe—which is the one in which most lay people think they reside—as being the actual universe. Even the universe of the mid-twentieth century physicists, as yet a foreign place to most of its inhabitants, is equally unreal and equally in process of redefinition.

What then is to be thought of man? How is he to evaluate himself? What methods and materials can he use? He has turned his shiny instruments inward on his own kind, eager to identify new aspects by which he can be described, delighted at the prospect of reducing himself to simple units of a modern sort. Yet a good deal of contemporary analytic work is not of a type which provides adequate conceptions of human nature. Analysis is pleasant work, to be sure. It is the kind of thing which must be done in order to make available a diversity of facts. It ought to be done by people who enjoy it, and they should be paid enormous salaries for doing it because by and by they will be old and may never have had the satisfaction of knowing anything that is of general significance. There certainly ought to be some variety of compensation for the misfortune of expending one's life on small matters.

Knowing, it has been suggested, is generally operational in character. While control of the natural world is common enough to cause no comment or remark, already the age of science defined as a distinctive way of knowing seems to have come to a subtle end. As has been noted elsewhere, in the 1952 Bampton Lectures at Columbia University, *Modern Science and Modern Man,* James B. Conant recorded his conviction that scientific and other-than-scientific kinds of knowing should no longer be separately defined, but should be recognized as one process. This is a decision of some significance in the long journey of the mind, the implications of which may take some time to see. It is as if a sandbar had been building below the surface for a long time, and at this point had shoaled, leaving in the history of thought the quiet surface of an oxbow to mark a former course while the main stream moved more swiftly on its way.

After a lapse of centuries individual human life appears once more at the center of the physical universe, returning to a position from which man was demitted in the enthusiasms of great discoveries pointing far afield. He is restored to this post because without his occupation of it there is neither order nor substance in himself or his environment; without him it is not clear whether there is so much as chaos. Even in his absence any available meanings are seen to be residual from his erstwhile presence. Man's centrality in nature also restores to a controlling position in the relief map of personality the concepts of mind and of interior, sustaining human nature. If man stands at the center of nature, mind stands at the center of man, actively defining what is to be known and the forms in which it is known. Imperial mind forever calls the turn of what the mind shall know.

If the human situation is to be encompassed, the search for understanding must be carried to the source, or at least to the gateway of the source: the mind must ask questions of itself, and in the effort to understand the rest of nature must pose very much larger and more comprehensive questions. The answers to the questions will of necessity be tentative, perhaps not very informative or durable; but that is to be expected and is quite all right. The late Dean Willard Sperry of the Harvard Divinity School used to say that the evidence concerning the nature of things was not all in and that conclusions would have to be drawn hesitantly instead of firmly for a long time to come. Actually this will probably be the case indefinitely. Conclusions will insist on modifying themselves at intervals, forming patterns which will serve only until new conceptions force a change of view.

How then shall the judgmental process take place? Judgments and choices, decisions involving commitment to values, often to be made on the basis of some selection of evidence, constantly present their cases for disposition. How are these to be settled? And by what criterion shall the large category of incomplete judgments be counterpoised? The comment which comes to mind may be an obvious one, readily missed by virtue of its familiar presence. Individual mind must simply judge the evidence as best it can, freed by its awareness of its definitive role in understanding from exclusive dependence upon image and measurement of limited scope. The consensus of experience and insight must provide the basis of judgment—which may not seem to be saying very much and yet in repeating the obvious does also confirm the confidence in the ordinary individual and his capacities which have to be assumed if the conception of man is not to be obscured by his social components. To make clear the historical dimension of experience and insight, insofar as clarity of experience and insight have been derivable from history, may be the task of tradition at its best, ancient wisdom resurgent in new forms.

The dilemma of subjectivism run wild may intrude itself into the problem of judgment. Is reliable judgment possible at all under some conditions? Can the self be so insulated by its lack of contact with all but the external aspects of things, or so deceived by its assignment of names to the sensations it receives that it cannot hope to know more than the "signs" of things? A conceptual approach such as the present one posits the effective grasp of reality, if not completely in the depth dimension (which would be a good deal to expect, surely), then at least to a degree not subject to a nominalistic reservation. This is, as has been noted, an assertive position. Mind commands attention to selected parts of the curved complexity of its surroundings. These are certainly parts and not wholes, but perceptions in depth may be more or less complete and subject to development or withdrawal depending on whether a given dimension of understanding is advanced or diminished. Subjectivist schools represent explorations of the potentialities of the self operating in partial vacuums, solely on its own batteries, so to speak, subsisting without relationships or responsibilities, attempting to see whether it can function without reference to the world outside. Secular existentialist schools are often of considerable psychological interest but otherwise have little future of their own and in time will burn themselves out, leaving at best a slight residual knowledge of the potential of the self-subsisting personality of man. The "beat" cults are in a state one step removed beyond these; the secular existentialists care, and earnestly try to solve problems, while the "beat" cults do not care, and do not try much of anything. They represent mind stricken with total poverty of meaning, personality sitting feebly in the smoke, stroking and oiling itself somewhere apart from the world's work. This is concern with the self gone utterly to seed, a kind of parasitic semi-consciousness. But these are minor aberrations. The reflective person need not be misled by cultural side-issues and pinwheels. Major issues and general ideas are far more powerful and of far greater interest. Beatnik cults no doubt help to define the lesser phases of personality, but their personal and social costs are too high and they will disappear. The general picture is that of mind by its nature engaged in the effort to understand the multi-dimensional universe, having at its disposal myriad possible vectors, selectable theoretically at will but actually limited by the conceptual self-restraints of a given culture. Conceptual freedom is the doorway on the universe. To conceptions wisely based, corresponding parts of the outside world are real, as other parts may be to other minds. Mind may therefore judge as best it can, proceeding honorably on the ground of what it knows.

The Strange and Stubborn Soul

The reflective observer is in a dilemma. The sciences of man imply a view of man's nature which is not adequate as a general conception of personality and human life. Yet it may be necessary for systematic investigation to work from partial conceptions in order to study aspects of the subject which ought to be described. The contemplative observer must then recognize the services which the sciences perform, while in general terms declining to believe what they say. For the sciences have developed through purposeful limitations of ideas and methods and the supposedly general implications produced by this approach may also be limited.

Inevitably, any asserted view of man will be incomplete, restricted by the range of ideas and methods which enable it. But if the reflective mind brings to bear what information it can, shaped by what wisdom it possesses, there will be at least a philosophic entity in place of the piles of conceptual slabwood which too often obscure the heart of the matter. Conceptual assertion will also be governed by past judgments re-judged as well as by broad contemporary perspectives.

In an effort to characterize individual human nature in an appropriate way and to recognize the restored integrity of human life defined as independent unit of conceptual substance we may revive the general notion of the soul. Some years ago Professor Hocking observed with the aptness which marks all his writings that the soul of man "is simply the human self in its dealings with its total horizon, trying to hold its bearings in the infinite universe of fact and meaning." To retain its bearings, he continues, or to recover them if they are lost is for the soul a matter of life and death, and it is not likely to recover them without acknowledging its own nature. And the fact is that man's nature will not find its self-completion in the ministrations of society. And why not? On every side one hears how social a creature man is and how much of his personality is given to him by other men. Yet there appears to be about his nature an element of originality which strives to organize its learnings, and which to do so can best make use of reference points outside its orders of conceptual familiarity. Landmarks of reference are frequently set up within the conceptional orders to serve as pivot points of idea systems without unnecessarily dragging in some primal cause. But these efforts are never really successful, never completely satisfying. They are again the partial descriptions which help to describe a totality but never encompass it. They are human constructs, and are subject to the limitations of any devised form. The soul of man can outreach any form it can create. This is the main insight of the religious existentialists, who present a special awareness of the capacity of the human spirit to range beyond particular forms, and so to the precision of new forms beyond which in turn it moves again. Eventually, to answer the endless query which makes of life the quest it cannot help but be, the soul must stand outside its own orders of existence; it must find its peace in the existence of God.

Man is therefore far more than a huddled coil sheltering from the drumbeats of sensation, responding only as he must when one of his prefabricated circuits is triggered off by a bit of cosmic flotsam. He is more, too, than a bundle of sluice-ways through which the circling impulses of natural process find temporary channel. He is more than a fleeting circumscription of the bare impulses themselves from the brief configurations of which even the hard paths have been peeled away. Nor can he be considered a sudden constellation of pauses in the welter of physical process, the patterns of which somehow constitute a total person until in the normal course its little elements fly off again about their business. Similarly, the materials of the social sciences are unable to provide the grounds for a general description of human nature. The complexity of an individual life can hardly be reconstructed out of the sharp remarks of its ancestors dredged up by the professional counselors of middle age; it cannot consist of the colors of a schoolgirl's dress remembered from long ago, or, in more statistical and more reputable terms, of the density of population in the region of one's childhood home. Such thin aspects of life do not take us very far toward a comprehensive conception of human nature.

The nature of man is difficult to deny. It can be fooled for a few centuries if it is kept busy enough. It has a tendency to feel that it has reached the truth because what it is doing is so time-consuming or the results so obvious. Activity alone, however, will not do. In time the old questions of meaning will reassert themselves. Then in the realm of ideas there must be a period of large construction, enabled by the stretching of the mind to the farther reaches of significance. The concepts may be temporary and need re-formation at some later time. That will take care of itself; mind can grasp what it should grasp. It is restricted only by the limits of its daring, by the weakness of the ideas with which it starts. To study man one must first have a view of man, and to study him effectively one must first have effective conceptions of his nature.

In this instance the nature of man is described as an instrument of vast conceptual reach, but also as an instrument which all too readily can run amok like the soulless monsters of the fiction mills, that have no hearts but only brains and are somehow inexplicably evil. Man is in decidedly better case. Yet he imprisons himself in the happy misery of knobs and gadgets unless he invites his mind and heart to wander hand in hand as his very soul among the farthest and the nearest reaches of the universe, where the sharp conceptual thrust cannot follow, there being no forms to serve as guides. It is as if man could not achieve his full stature until he had striven toward the than-which-nothing-greater-can-be-conceived, that penumbral foreshadowing of the inconceivable to which the deep-feeling religious existentialist attempts to apply the seventh sense, which the secular existentialist tries to describe in some form even while having no reason to bother with it other than simple curiosity. Man by himself loses his bearings. He may subsist for a time on the momentum of inherited vectors. He may forget his predicament by keeping very busy, or he may accept one of the numerous substitutes for God. But he will have at best an interim satisfaction and in the end he or his descendants will dwell with the Giant Despair. The confusions of the age and the turmoil of heart which they engender, as well as the ways in which the soul finds peace, affirm the nature of man as reflection of Divinity.

Ultimate Moral Choice

Empiricism being an illusion, the first requirement of functioning human nature is not an external stimulus but an idea in terms of which to establish personal and social direction. Human nature has potential for good and evil; it can undertake to be encouraged in either direction. The liberal view of the goodness of personality, accurate beyond question in many settings, has been delimited by the implications of enormous cruelties contrived on immense scales. Human nature is indeed capable of festering in its own evil. In the search for meaning which is part of the life of every man there is a directional choice to be made in terms of a point of reference defined implicitly by active tendencies if not also explicitly by reason. The final decision must at heart be a moral one which each man must make as best he can, for which he may if he wishes summon the wisdom of the ages as well as the experience of present times to assist in the judgment of good and evil. At this point the distinction between metaphysics and ethics disappears; conduct is intrinsically articulated with belief; theory and practice, ideal and actual, supposition and realization, all are one.

Moral choice in this degree is a movement toward the ultimate. It is perhaps a decision to establish an operating conception of man's nature bent toward the highest objectives which experience and inspiration have shown to be possible. Clearly, no dog-leash variety of human nature will come close to fulfilling the implied demand for dignity and responsibility among men. It is at this point that the Invisible Man, long hidden and long forgotten, moves slowly out of the shadows, not as in the story at the moment of his dying, but alive and on the verge of life magnificent.

II The Philosophy of Knowledge

From time to time in the history of thought the philosophic center of gravity shifts, perhaps only by a little when all is said and done, but still it shifts, and there are consequences for education and for ideas. The purpose of this review will be to move back and forth among the implications of such a shift at the present time to see what meaning it may have for reflective thought and for the direction of education in the contemplative fields.

By way of premise it is suggested that the fundamental element in human motivation is the urge to know. The will to knowledge can be broadly defined as antecedent to all the organic hungers. A case can undoubtedly be made for the moral dimension as fundamental on higher levels and this possibility should be left open for future consideration. For the time being, however, one may settle on what appears universal for life in general. Major fields of knowledge, as philosophy, religion and the sciences, then become developments in the main theme and may be seen in varied perspective. In the 20th century, moreover, intentional judgment has been increasingly applied to common problems in an effort to improve the conditions of life. It will be wise to apply judgment in the reaches of reflective thought as well, rather than to regard the contemplative interests merely as diversions of the idle mind. Who is to say that an effective world-view is not a vital condition of personal and social well-being?

On the Nature of Knowing

American thought is marked, perhaps even more than European, by periodic fracture of established conceptions of objective reality. It is as if the mood of individualism could not endure confinement for long within a shell of ideas representing an external world to which one does not contribute but only responds. The construction of objective patterns seems to deny freedom to the originality which devised them. Yet human nature constantly demands just such patterns, and so the merry round goes on.

Among the many philosophic currents which flow in a given age there is now a movement away from a view of the world as objective toward emphasis on the role of the individual in perceiving that world. If the universe outside the self is hard and fast, irreducible, ultimate, waiting only to be discovered, man can do little except learn to live more cleverly within its iron frame. If on the other hand life contributes through its perceptions to the substance and selection of the universe, the situation of subject and object becomes suddenly fluid; the conceptions of human nature and of the world-external stand open to revision. This is the present case.

Restriction of this trend to consideration of internal states and feelings will result in a series of truncated subjectivisms of "existential" types as have been common in recent years. If working relationships are recognized between subject and object, however, knowledge may be of several effective kinds—photographic, filtered, or sliced thin. The individual may even be left alone in the dark with only the signs of things for company, where the very daylight is a species of deceit having no value except that of constancy in its deception. This, too, is knowledge of a kind, for the individual can operate reliably in his remote condition, albeit not unlike the expert in rare elements whose bloodless fingers, fixed to the ends of poles, pour liquid fire fresh from the vitals of the universe.

The subjective emphasis is open to many types of error, and several of these have been put forward in the century since Kierkegaard and Hegel. Yet surely it is desirable for the role of the perceiver to be worked through in this stage, with reference to the composition of human nature and available facets of the natural world. A new formulation of the process of knowing may be in order, to balance a new fusion of conceptions of reality regrettably separated some centuries ago.

Recognition of the conceptual nature of knowing as common to science, philosophy and religion raises implications significant for reflective studies at the college level. Disconcerting ideas crowd in upon the mind. The philosophic centre of gravity abruptly shifts, temporarily perhaps, from the external world to the world within. No longer is attention directed primarily outward among the neutrons and the nebulae, and only secondarily inward on man's nature—his nature, incidentally, as child of the hairy ape. Rather the focus falls first on the nature of man in all its unconfinable complexity, and through it becomes free to center upon phases of the outside world selected by interests of the mind.

Mind becomes of pivotal importance. Far from being merely the echo of chemical traffic roaring among the nerves, or the by-product of biological events reflected in evanescent media, mind becomes the signalman of the human system, independent centre of judgment and communication, the unit of individual life which at once provides access to the metaphysical depths of existence and direction for the earnest outreach of the soul.

Empiricism is seen to be at best a momentary phenomenon, erroneous in its findings and existing if at all only for minute fractions of time when transitions from pattern to pattern and age to age may permit brief consideration of unselected fact. Knowing in general is not of this order. It requires organization; organization requires principle; and principle follows upon activity of mind. Intelligible knowledge is ultimately constructional in nature, and only incidentally or methodologically analytic. Physical analysis remains a useful tool; it ought not to be considered in its reductionist aspect fundamental in the construction of comprehensive theories of environment and life. Understanding follows upon assertive activity of mind; intellective assertion enables discovery and selection of identifiable facets of reality. Knowledge cannot be confined to the results of analytic minutism, but requires recognition that human life, existing presumably in a middle range of perceptual possibility, functions on the basis of conceptions which have subjective and objective standing on their given levels. Consequences for the validity of universals may follow, though the issue at the moment is not germane.

Religion and Science as Forms of Knowing

Knowing is one thing in all the major fields of concern. Connections are established of some import for religion and science, and bearing upon their consideration in systematic studies.

When all is said and done, that which religion has striven to do since earliest times has been to place mankind in an effective operating relationship with the powers of the universe. Physical and spiritual well-being are end functions of cognitive activity. Man's ceaseless striving to know his world is his preeminent characteristic. Theories and patterns have taken many forms but their common purpose has not changed. A world-view places the individual in a recognizable context, that he may live with assurance amid the mysteries of his time. There are other concerns in religion but they are related to this—the will to know where one stands and to stand where one knows.

And when all is similarly said and done, the concern to know the universe and to cast mankind in proper role within it is also the primary problem of the sciences. It is perhaps fair to say that the enormous scientific activity of this age derives in part from convenient discoveries of practices and techniques the working out of which produce desirable conditions of life and varied conceptions of certain of its aspects. The underlying faith of the sciences, as Burtt and Whitehead and others have remarked, is the faith of the Middle Ages that the world is reliable and can be known and that man is capable of knowing it. The direction of attention toward the phenomena of this world perceived through the senses, surely a characteristic of a "scientific" age and greatly cherished by the modern mood, is seen to be akin to the mediaeval realism of St. Thomas Aquinas and ultimately to the Aristotelian shift from the idea to the thing. Science as a general human activity must be concerned in a philosophic way with questions of significance, unless it is to be meaningless motion or a dead thrashing, and so it is, like many other cultural phases, related to the religious root, tied to it by the nature of its work and its methods of procedure.

In these two fields the procedures of knowing are strictly held in common; there is no marked difference between the knowing of science and the knowing of religion. Each type involves construction or grasp of conceptual patterns against which perceived materials are checked. More than this, constructional concepts enable far-reaching advances in understanding. While from time to time systems of ideas have become old and restrictive and therefore subject to assault, by their nature they have enabled in the first instance the splendid achievements of the mind which have changed the face of nature and greatly deepened man's understanding of his habitation. There is the memorable passage in Whitehead's *Science and the Modern World* where he describes

> . . . the meeting of the Royal Society in London when the Astronomer Royal for England announced that the photographic plates of the famous eclipse, as measured by his colleagues in

Greenwich Observatory, had verified the prediction of Einstein that rays of light are bent as they pass in the neighborhood of the sun. The whole atmosphere of tense interest was exactly that of the Greek drama: we were the chorus commenting on the decree of destiny as disclosed in the development of a supreme incident. There was dramatic quality in the very staging: — the traditional ceremonial, and in the background the picture of Newton to remind us that the greatest of scientific generalizations was now, after more than two centuries, to receive its first modification. Nor was the personal interest wanting: a great adventure in thought had at length come safe to shore.

Where apparent conflicts of religion and science have occurred, as in the century of Copernicus and Galileo and later in the times of Darwin and Thomas Huxley, they have been disagreements of a conceptual order, of interpretation, rather than conflicts of "dogma" and "fact" as often supposed. At the time of its inception Copernican theory was less an appeal to sensory fact than a theoretical construction devised to account for larger numbers of facts than were subsumed under earlier theories. To its contemporaries it was a contradiction of evidences from the senses (obviously the sun went around the earth), and the conflicts it engendered were conflicts of habits of mind. So it was with theories of evolution and of divine creation in the later period.

The warfare of religion and the sciences, pursued with such good will in the recent century, has therefore had an illusory character. It has not entailed much actual disagreement over what is real, though it may have seemed to do so. Alleged conflicts of science and religion have been disputes of phases of thought under conditions in which the respective time-stages have been ignored. The perspective on intellectual change has been too short for the nature of the disagreements to be clear. A more accurate relationship can be discovered in the common purposes of religious and scientific thought—determination of the nature of life and its setting, and in the apparent identity of their procedures of knowing. The coinage remains the same for all parts of the realm.

To be sure, the shouting of Huxley against the bishops had its uses in the long view. Periodically the accustomed patterns of thought must be broken up, and this Huxley did on behalf of Darwin who rested at home with his headaches, rejoicing in the sounds of arms from afar. The curious thing is that conceptual change of this kind commonly appears to be greater than it really is. A minor shift of emphasis from one variety of conceptual assumption to another is seen as a movement of far-reaching scope and significance, as altering ways of thinking and as changing the character of the total universe. That the actual change in outlook is very slight and the shift in the perceivable aspect of nature is largely illusory or at most a movement among aspects, suggests that the implications of intellectual history tend to be misunderstood. Similarly, the general climate of opinion obtaining at a given time is seen as differing remarkably from the climates of other times, and the transitions between them are examined with a closeness which tends to overrate their metaphysical importance. The major changes between one age of thought and another most often derive from removal of general interest from one set of philosophic questions to another, with the consequence that different aspects of reality become prominent at different times. It does not follow that the nature of objective reality is altered decisively merely because the focus of investigative attention is moved, or that some earlier set of questions will not be restated in some new form, perhaps periodically, when the problems which they represent again become immediate.

Educational patterns in the contemplative fields have been shaped in part by classifications developed as agents of convenience under conditions no longer familiar. Traditional divisions in philosophy, science and religion continue to yield useful results, but they must make place for values deriving from general ideas and from perspectives unusually long.

The traditional fields have in common the original concern of human life, the urge to know, a concern which underlies even the will to live since it must precede the satisfaction of hungers as well as the lacework of less demanding interests. Each of the three fields relies on that form of conceptual thought which marks every endeavor of intellectual man. The same conceiving power selects aspects of nature for perception and study and so reveals the gifts of comprehension and control which inhere in the mind.

For educational purposes many studies are useful and few can be condemned. To concentrate, however, on general questions thrown up by existence, insofar as that is desirable, attention may center on conceptual world-views of the largest compass, those remarkable schemas by which men have pictured to themselves the worlds in which they lived, and in so doing have at once discovered and created them.

The Philosophy of Knowledge

As distinguished, then, from analytic epistemology, the philosophy of knowledge will be concerned with conceptual prehensions of reality in all ages and cultures, and in whatever disciplines they may be found. Cosmology alone is too limited a field to comprise a philosophy of knowledge, but it would be a vital ingredient and perhaps a first approach. The content of a college study in this region of the mind would vary with individual interests, drawing on assertive systems from classical, mediaeval and modern times. Reading could be drawn from Biblical and Greek sources, the Church Fathers, mediaeval reflections through Aquinas and Dante, and from standard early modern and contemporary figures. Scientific thought in recent centuries, selections from the several fields through the 19th century, religious philosophy and the supposedly secular systems—all would offer exciting possibilities. Reviews and research in the history of thought would provide helpful over-views, while a variant approach by way of the philosophers of history also suggests itself. Views of Eastern cultures should stand with those of the West. These fields and their principal figures are familiar ground in many disciplines and are not unusual as they appear in this connection. It is perhaps the focus and the point of view, the kind of question asked and the answers sought, which will serve to organize a philosophy of knowledge.

Experience in history would have its values, but studies in conceptual schemas would in addition respond to the needs of contemporary thought. Comprehensive conceptions of reality, of nature and human life, are of immense significance in the present age. The determinative role of metaphysical assumption cannot wisely be ignored, though in recent times it has been almost replaced by a childlike and carefree running up and down of philosophic alleys. Sharply curtailed perspectives of metaphysical kinds have in turn restricted conceptions of the self and its capacities. Its powers of reflective construction have been reduced by limitations of conviction, its destructive powers relatively strengthened by fascination with its animal inheritance. However, contemplative asseveration, lately considered a light-weight game of the mind, resumes its old insistence and overflows into ethical and social realms. The consequences for self-confidence and self-direction and for social behavior on a wide scale need no elaboration. Surely at this point the relation between the popular metaphysics and the ethico-social conduct of large groups of people comes into the clear. Eventually one must encounter that silent metaphysics-of-the-people to which so much of individual and group behavior is a response, and of which the precise versions of the scholars are merely developed variations.

Students of college age, coming to reflective studies when ultimate questions are especially poignant, should become accustomed to thinking in large terms and should be familiar with the classical efforts by which ancient and modern figures have described their several worlds. Conceptual studies will serve these purposes, among others. The entrance of new minds into the fields of reflection and assertion may help to answer the conceptual needs of the world's populations. New data will constantly be discovered; new relationships of data must constantly be clarified. Frames of reference must be built and built again to set off accumulating information. Widening perspectives are in strong demand.

Implied here is a deliberate shift of the weight of contemplation in some parts of college study, adding to the analytic and comparative emphases the concern for synthesis and constructional thought. Specific programs of study in the philosophy of knowledge will be traditional and perhaps commonplace for teachers in many fields. What may be different is the focus and direction, the determination to expend deliberate effort in the construction of worldviews, in assertion of general ideas to account for the characteristics and setting of life. Individual mind creates its counterpoise from facets of the endless universe. The conduct of life depends for its wisdom on the arch of meaning between the self and its aspects of reality. Mind adventures, and the world, if it will, responds. When the leap is made and the balance met, there is fulfillment; when part is lost, there is confusion or the fall.

The contemplative fields of thought have traditionally dealt with this problem. The sciences have preferred to engage in happy voyages of discovery, supposing that were simpler. Yet clearly, no one of the investigative fields can do without the organizing principles of reflection. Even the sciences have taken up their philosophic implications, albeit too often confined to picking at inconsequential matters well out in the suburbs of significance. Actually, the sciences have always stood closely with philosophy in the implications—drawn or not—of positions they have wished to take, as Burtt has shown in his *Metaphysical Foundations of Modern Physical Science*. Few recognitions can be more helpful than that ultimate questions pervade every phase of man's existence, tower over every field of thought, demand in eloquent silence answers which every field of study finally wills to give.

The philosophy of knowledge then comes over on several levels. It provides for historical studies of conceptual schemas, in part for the methods and materials of other days and in part for the breadth of awareness involved in the discipline. At the same time it lives acutely in the present, reconstructing comprehensions of nature and life as required by an age buried beneath mounting piles of factual shards and rubble. By implication the philosophy of knowledge throws open for re-study the nature of subject and object and the problem of communication between the two.

The concern of education for these reaches of philosophy is a function of its inescapable relation to metaphysics—that is, to its total view of the world as conceived to be real. When method predominates in education it does so usually on the basis of metaphysical assumptions which require careful examination, or, more commonly, for convenience in resolving community needs in situations where general ideas are not at issue.

A single process of knowing underlies religion, philosophy, the sciences, and education. Their respective appearances are not greatly changed; their vectors face in various directions; they continue to function in different ways. Still, the shadows of these great fields of endeavor are cast toward a common concern. Forthwith the present age is seen to dwell on the edge of a conceptual volcano.

III Kierkegaard's Judgment; The Attack Upon Christendom

It speaks well for western communions that Kierkegaard's attack upon Christendom has been accepted with as much humility and fair grace as it has. For various reasons the work by that name has not been as available or as widely read as the earlier works, or as well considered. But churchmen have been willing to face its implications, acknowledging their own susceptibility to error and failure, granting that the establishment of the kingdom of God on earth is not a simple outcome of good intentions, even the good intentions of the consecrated life.

Nevertheless, when a prophet of religious experience, albeit one who always dwelt apart, after a decade of devotion to the study of the pilgrim's way turns openly against the church and its leaders, surely so strange an address asks justifiable questions. Churchmen could be forgiven if they resumed their labors in some bewilderment, uncertain how far to condemn themselves for being human.

Old Bishop Mynster had died in January 1854. A distinguished public figure, Primate of the Danish Church for many years, friend of Kierkegaard's father, the aging bishop had commanded general respect. While he lived, Kierkegaard honored him at least with silence and held his peace. But the movement of his thought was clear enough. When the Bishop died and Pastor Martensen who was to succeed him in office memorialized him as a witness to the truth, a genuine Christian in the apostolic line, the transgression for Kierkegaard was irretrievable. From December of 1854 to September of 1855 the reading public was treated to a series of editorial diatribes in pamphlets and periodicals, attacking the late patriarch, attacking Pastor Martensen whom Kierkegaard disliked and who represented to him the rampant evils of formal religiosity and ecclesiasticism, and through these, attacking also the church, the clergy, and popular adherence to an expression of religion which seemed to be only a mocking imitation. His burden was that a true Christian must give up the world, deny the particular and the universal planes of life, respond only to the call of the infinite which like the horn of Roland winds through the mountains as if from a great distance. No bishop or formal churchman, no conventional Christian, Kierkegaard felt, could do this. His situation and commitments would prevent it. The wandering pilgrim alone could decline the world and in taking leave of it become more truly Christian.

The effect of Kierkegaard's attack was predictable. Public interest in his work fell away. When in October of 1855 he fell paralyzed in the street and lay dying for a month in the hospital at the age of 42, few friends remained to support him. After his death the eclipse extended to his earlier work. The negative impressions of the generations of his time would have to wear away before his insight could serve to deepen religious experience among theologians and general readers. *The Attack Upon Christendom* still stands as one of the puzzles of religious history. What could it mean?

The Idea and the Judgment

On the face of it, Kierkegaard's assault upon practical Christianity was an orderly derivation from his religious conviction. He had taken the position that life could not be lived in aesthetic terms without denying its ethical and religious demands. Sensation and its responses, this-worldliness, fulfillment of immediate vacancies and incompletenesses undertaken without consideration of conflicting demands of higher moral and religious imperatives—these could lead only to despair. Human nature is able to choose among several ways of life, but if it wills the lowest way its natural bent toward the better part will pass sentence upon itself—the sickness unto death.

Choice, continued Kierkegaard, is constant. The situations of life require the individual to make decisions. If he refuses to make them the situations will make them, throwing him aside as debris in the process he declined to enter. The pilgrim must choose, and by choice he must move into the ethical realm. There his life is lived in awareness of the relevance of ethical selection. Individual life no longer reacts in a simple way to the demands of immediacy or merely follows its impulses to particular fulfillments. Decision sets the individual on a new and formative path. His judgments are made with reference to universal principles. The relational dimension becomes controlling. In the Biblical story re-told in several ways in *Fear and Trembling* Abraham would once stay the knife because the conditions of common life require that murder be not committed. But this is not enough to reflect the demands and the possibilities of the human situation.

There remains in the religious realm the final confrontation of the soul in which the indescribable splendor of divinity is brought to bear on human existence. On this level the individual moves far ahead of the group. His awareness of truth is profound, if necessarily incomplete; his response to the ultimate is unilateral. Abraham knows that the nature of the decision has changed: the universal prohibition against murder does not apply. In its forward aspect the sacrifice is uni-dimensional, having in itself no horizontal or rearward relations. It has nothing to do with murder.

From this final stage, the realm of the religious, Kierkegaard implies a first juxtaposition of realms which ends in the bizarre. In drawing the contrast between the religious and the lesser realms he conveys a hypothetical turning about, a momentary retrogression of the mind disclosing a perspective beyond belief. It is as if, from a vantage point on a long journey, one gazed far back upon one's place of origin, sensing the distance come. Even the ethical realm, the highest kind of this-worldly life, marked by conscientious discrimination of good from evil on universal grounds, seems in its middle distance to be strangely remote. Its great accomplishments and its noble order have been suspended. This is the confrontation of the Infinite, bringing with it a suggestion of wholeness unqualified, of perspective unmarked by relative distances, of immensity of grasp beyond the reach of attributes and characteristics, a vision—a glimpse, perhaps—of that which is and may be.

Who can say if this was the vision of St. Thomas, the flashing insight which committed him to silence toward the end of his 49 years, making it impossible for him to add a single word to the volumes he had composed? From so great a height can the mind retain its ability to deal with the practical and ethical orders of existence? Was this why Aquinas retired to silence after so short and so full a life, and was this why he died? Is it not written that no man shall look upon the face of God and live? Perhaps some conceptions are large enough to split the mind. Perhaps Kierkegaard's vision was not quite complete, that he could look back at all on the way he had come, that he would live long enough to confuse the orders of existence.

To the dialectical triad of Hegel, with its systematic realization of Spirit in substance, process and life wholly accepted and acknowledged as real, Kierkegaard's reply was a directional plunge on the grand scale, rejective of life and process, selective of material and direction, a conceptual assertion circumscribed and channelled and therefore of great force. Kierkegaard's journey had already been long. His judgment upon Christendom was a judgment upon the here-and-now from a reference point apart from space and time. As an absolute judgment on a finite subject it was necessarily a dislocation. It may have had uses, but in its own precise terms it had no relevance and could have no effect.

The incompleteness of Kierkegaard's conceptual adventure also bears on the problem. The frenetic search for the religious idea in the practical world and the anger engendered by the failure to find it are comments more upon the situation of the seeker than upon the object of the search and its supposed location in the practical world, the emptiness of which is proverbial and not at issue. An attack mounted upon the finite from the standpoint of the near-infinite is a declaration of uncertainty as to the nature of the infinite. The attack to the rear is part of the quest, bumbling and misdirected, but part of the quest. The realm of the finite should never make the mistake of recognizing the attack except perhaps in the individual dimension. An attack in such perspective is emphatically not an appropriate comment upon the immediate, which subsists as required and is only unfairly brought under fire for not being other than it is ordered to be.

Kierkegaard's Dilemma

One may say, a judgment from the absolute may not be made upon a finite subject as the finite and infinite are by definition wholly different and do not communicate. But the present age is not sufficiently at home with reason to be content with a logical resolution of the issue. The point to be made is that a judgment applied to the finite may be finite itself although remote in perspective and origin, or that it may be truly an absolute judgment and therefore inapplicable to the finite even though by terminology and intention it may appear to be so. The problem is one of communication and understanding. How can a judgment be effective if its degree of removal from its object is so great that there is no possibility of its being understood, no chance of its being taken account of by the immediacy on which it bears?

This was Kierkegaard's problem. The origin of his judgment was in religious understanding, immensely remote in a qualitative sense, and its content, whether or not it was absolute, surely surpassed the rational and partook of the divine. The judgment was made in the light of advanced religious insight, but the object of the judgment was immediate. The contemporary church of his day could not be the repository of the Word, Kierkegaard thought, nor could its leaders be true witnesses for Christianity. Institutional and ecclesiastical life was stained by many kinds of self-concern, by prudence, by practicalities, by the necessities of organized and professional life. A figure immersed in a power situation could never realize the ideal, personally or professionally. His responsibilities and weaknesses will prove too much for him. Bishop Mynster could not have been a Christian for he remained within the world. No man could be a Christian and remain within the world. How does one know? By knowing that the way of the Christian is renunciation of particular and universal, an approach toward the religious. No Christian could remain with the crowd. Where the crowd is, there is not-Christianity. To be a Christian one must be alone with one's different belief or one's deeper grasp of the common belief. Bishop Munster was not alone; he too could not be a Christian. In Kierkegaard's terms the conclusion is clear enough. The finite is not the infinite; the partial falls short of being the absolute; the realms of the immediate cannot partake of the religious. What could be clearer? Kierkegaard's judgment was right.

Kierkegaard's judgment was right, but was Kierkegaard right? The religious ideal, to be sure, was not realized in the domain of the church. But what could be done about it? What can ever be done about it? Should Bishop Mynster die again, from shame? Should Bishop Martensen retire from office and cease to function? What can a man do? One sins and falls short. One is selfish and concerned for tomorrow. One must resolve problems in a power situation which one wishes one might not have to resolve, problems to which there can be only distressing and partial solutions.

Is not this the Christian problem and the religious problem? How shall the infinite speak to the finite, and how shall the finite reply? Suppose you are Bishop Mynster or Bishop Martensen, and you become the object of an absolute judgment. It can happen to anyone. What will you do? You will suffer, because, being no fool, you will know that the judgment is right. But what else will you do? If Kierkegaard looks back on the way he has come, if he speaks to his age from his point of view, he will have no choice as to what he will say. That is what perspective does. There will be nothing else to talk about, no other words to use. The content of the judgment will be right. The difficulty is that nothing at all can be done about it. What then is its relevance?

The Attack Upon Christendom

A judgment which partakes of the infinite at least serves to apply perspective to the finite. The finite realm may be incapable of significant response, except as sensitive individuals make individual response. It can perhaps become dissatisfied with itself and with its situation. Awareness of the infinite may create in the finite a sense of incompleteness, of despair. Solitary figures may from time to time detach themselves from it and move toward the infinite. Taking a long step toward the ultimate they cease to be a part of the finite and become unable to communicate effectively with it. They may comment on the finite, but aside from acknowledging the cutting edge of the criticism the finite as such can do nothing about it without ceasing to be.

The value of the absolute judgment thus far remains in its definition of conditions of the real to which the individual soul may respond out of its acute dissatisfaction. The positive aspect of the response will be a personal pilgrimage. But even this central idea of the Christian faith is restricted in scope, for some, like Bishop Mynster and Bishop Martensen, cannot concede a response and still continue in their appointed roles, and in addition to this Kierkegaard appears to define the way of salvation partly in terms of the rejection of salvation by most of the finite realm. The crowd can never be Christian; only the separative few can grasp and act upon the principles of faith.

How does the infinite speak to the finite? The notion of "tension" has been used to suggest that the absolute draws the finite out of itself, gives direction to the practical world, establishes a connection between it and the ideal. The content of tension is presumably a relation of awareness attended by moral demand. The assumption must be that awareness and the response to tension which derives from a moral imperative can and do make a difference. Perhaps some decisions in the practical realms can be made differently because of the suffering of non-fulfillment which goes with awareness of the infinite. But this kind of effect cannot be expected to alter the nature of the practical realms as such. Major or sudden changes on a large scale there could not be. Individual salvation remains the only way of escape from the finite toward the infinite, and in this view no significant alteration in the finite can occur apart from individual withdrawal and re-direction of the self, an idea which, conceived as the way of salvation, lies at the heart of Christian conviction.

The church by definition operates in the realms of the finite, sometimes in the aesthetic, sometimes in the universal, sometimes in both. This is its purpose and its proper function as a mediating entity. No doubt it is unjust to expect the church to embody the absolute in its life and work, for it could not do so without terminating its institutional existence. Nor are the lives of priests and clergy subject to review in absolute terms, for they too must perform in the realms of the finite and are therefore not free to respond to the call of the infinite without ceasing to be of use in the immediate situation. Like Moses before the land of Canaan the professional clergy must stand aside from the higher life, assisting other men to go where as yet they may not go, forgetful of self until in the goodness of time and the ripeness of years their call will come.

Kierkegaard's judgment on the church had of necessity to be a confusion of orders of existence. He could speak of the finite only in finite terms, making use of its materials, forms, and procedures. But his judgment was from the near-infinite even while his words were the names of the finite. The content of his attack could have nothing to do with its subject. The perspective of the infinite could not bear upon the substance of the finite. That his attack went wide of the mark was inevitable; it could not be otherwise, for that which he addressed was not where he thought it was. Kierkegaard's cannonade was aimed at a mirage—which reflected the particular in every way and yet was far from it because it could be associated conceptually with the perspective of the infinite. Such a mistake could never be made with the actual finite. Kierkegaard lobbed his shells a world away. They exploded without relevance, their brief turbulence engulfed at once in the shimmering image. By the prevalent misfortune of language wherein a given term is ordinarily understood in a given way, Kierkegaard's audience supposed that he really meant what he said. In reality he did not because he could not. The idea which he strove to express could not be expressed in words; and the words which the paucity of conception and language forced him to use ended by playing him false. They embodied a meaningless attack. It was as if two worlds slipped past one another helplessly in space.

He presented the infinite, the perspective of divinity, to the finite world insofar as a living man is able to do. He did what he could. But he might as well have carried the burning sun in a handbasket. Failing this, he had then to choose silence. If he chose to speak he could only condemn the indefensible for there was nothing else to say, and there were no other words or terms to use. Kierkegaard's meaning lay not in his words but behind them in the silence out of which he spoke. The words were not what he was saying, and there were no words for what he meant.

His hearers would understand, in a dumb way, for it is a rare soul that does not know its weakness. But no one would be able to do anything in response to it other than to undertake the personal withdrawal from the finite, and most of the clergy could not even do that. Salvation of the soul is an individual affair; it is not the affair of an entire realm of the finite, nor yet of the finite individual whose consecration is to the service of the finite in the midst of its populous wastes.

Kierkegaard's ultimate judgment on the aesthetic and the ethical realms is therefore bizarre—possibly even embarrassing, injurious, destructive on those levels—above all, bizarre. He pointed the way of the pilgrim which few could take. He had then, like St. Thomas, to fall silent, awaiting the fullness of vision which would be both end and beginning.

IV Existentialisms as Interstices

Philosophic studies are supposed to be heavy with intellect, distant from the drives and wells of feeling. It is not so. Philosophies are full of mystery. They are grounded in mystery and they conclude in mystery, and if they give the impression of relative clarity it is only because earnest philosophers scrabble busily about their woods and pastures picking up twigs and mowing buttercups, keeping everything in eager order.

Of course the order does not last and does not extend very far. John Haynes Holmes liked to tell of his efforts to control his summer yard far down on the coast of Maine or New Brunswick. His compost piles of weeds and trimmings grew larger year after year, but the victories were passing. Each season the clearing had all to be done again. Nor need one visit the northeast coast to learn the homely truth: how many well-intentioned gardeners have been compelled by the burdens of affairs to raise their weed-ceilings from ten to thirty inches?

Philosophies are not so very different from this. They can get their premises straight for the moment and can even project a number of useful lines out into chaos. From a certain standpoint this constitutes the attainment of reflective order, and one might inadvisedly rejoice in possession of a finished system. But give it twenty minutes from any aeon and the entire complex will drift away with its lines and curls awash like a jellyfish in a sea-wind.

A major mystery in philosophic studies is where new reflective positions originate. Genealogies of ideas are useful but are valid primarily in their own terms; when detached from cultural contexts the inheritances they trace may be dubious at best, and the implied manner of transmission seriously in error. The ''influence'' which ideas and persons are said to have had on other ideas and persons suggests direct relation; frequent studies are made of sources of ideas, the readings of philosophers in their youth, and the teachers with whom they may have worked in early years. Material of this kind is indeed of absorbing interest but it should be understood comprehensively so that the abstraction is metaphysically full-bodied and of the nature of idea. An aspect-abstraction does not possess enough ground to bear usefully on the question. The transmission of ideas is better understood in terms of resonance; direct transmission could account for only a very small part of philosophic position-taking. The happier relations of teacher and student are then constructed largely out of the pleasures of recognition and encouragement. The notion of resonance provides the metaphysical and interpersonal base for educational communication.

Teaching can then be different things at different times. In a period when a strong current of ideas has begun to run philosophic motion may consist in very limited part of didactic transmission, but only in part and for very brief periods; and even then, if there is insufficient allowance for originality and innovation the forces of philosophic life will merely break the molds the sooner. In general, teaching in the reflective fields will in the first instance consist of looking about to see what students are thinking. Cultural situations and stages of development have then a great deal to do with the nature of teaching in particular periods.

It is as if the great currents of reflective thought were subterranean in nature, a vast underground concourse of rivers, winding among caverns, thundering into hidden cataracts or swiftly flowing in darkness and silence, each current awaiting the geologic circumstance which allows it to emerge for time to sparkle among sunlit meadows until in the normal course it descends again to give place to other streams.

What Are Existentialists Doing?

Existential philosophy is on the standard baggage list of students leaving home for college in these days. They meet it in high school classes along with goofballs and the literature of protest, so that each new group of college students walking on campus for the first time brings with it what passes for the newest and most modern stance. Existentialism is thought to be the residual purity left over when the encrusted clap-trap of the mind has been cast over the cliff; in its exhilarating renewal the seeker can stand free of the burdensome past, face forward squarely, ruffling his hair in the fresh winds of morning.

Maritain has of course shown that existentialism is not new at all, that it has been one of the persistent strands of Thomism for many centuries. Surely it represents one of the recurrent phases of reflective concern, one of the fundaments of a truly comprehensive philosophic system in any period in its complex involvement in the human self and the focus of the relations of the self with its surroundings. Major themes of thought can be recessive for long periods so that a facet which appears in a given time may be only unfamiliar rather than really new; or a theme may emerge newly re-combined with other elements, as existentialism is today with secularism or with the religiously derived psychiatric movement, and so take on an air of newness.

The function of the existentialist is to con himself for a good purpose. That is to say, to provide for orderly and periodic change in the envelope of ideas which gives meaning to existence there must occur denial of the old and affirmation of the new. The existentialist applies this necessity to his case by denying rational constructs in terms of which reality has been cast for a time and compensates by establishing a counter-ground. He would object to the handling of his positive position in ideological form since he begins by denying the idea-nature of his world-view; but perhaps this aspect of the matter can be put down to normal philosophic wear-and-tear without causing a metaphysical disaster. In the end the existentialist does have to be willing to think; he cannot indefinitely sit and grunt. If his thinking makes him over into something else that is a risk he must take. Stated otherwise, the existentialist's function is then to occupy himself with a philosophic phase or theme to the exclusion of other themes for the general purpose—which is not his own, necessarily—of reintroducing existential considerations into the modern matrix of reflective thought. He is self-deceived on the universality of his central concern, for it is on the contrary specialized and particularistic. But the same might be said of other reflective phases.

The existentialist then senses the rush of freedom when the old categories of understanding are gone, as if he had cut away bonds which had been holding him for a long time. Now at last he feels able to operate without obstruction over the full range of human possibility. Inevitably one is reminded of Winston Churchill's remarkable sigh of relief when he was appointed Prime Minister of England in May of 1940. He wrote in retrospect that he felt freed at last to give orders over the entire sweep of the great war just beginning to flame through Europe. Supreme trust in oneself is surely an existential phenomenon in whatever connection it appears.

Where shall the existentialist prospect for data? He must have data, for human nature requires knowledge. Might he be content with sensory evidence controllable by precise epistemological procedures as the positivist and the scientist are? He might be, but the literature shows that he is not. For his data even the secular existentialist looks within the human self, most immediately within his own particular self. His position requires him to look there first, hopefully, since in his view no evidence can be allowed to antedate the fact of his existence.

Even the term 'data' requires careful use. The positivist might turn out to be a better existentialist than the existentialist himself, as the existence of a life-unit, however defined, would antedate in an operational context the information on which his awareness of the external world must depend. He could restrict his orders of data to the phenomenological, and while his major position would be subject to normal assault on different premises within his own reference frame his position would be sound.

But we are not speaking of the positivist nor can we fall back on logic or systematic methodology. With existentialism we are speaking of habit. What existentialists do is read the self. From the raw materials of human nature, insofar as any judgment of the rest of the universe is made at all, the remainder of a world-view is extrapolated.

The religious existentialist is true to the prescription. He recognizes within his nature those threads of reality which come first in the structure of things; they are inevitably threads of the religious nature of existence. On the basis of these he can weave the web of reality which reflects the religious setting of existence in external phases as well, but notice that the evidence begins within the self. The religious philosopher who addresses his concern to Divinity and the relation of man to the ultimate conceived of as objective in relation to the self does so on the ground of principles or facets of the real to which he perceives his own nature to respond. Eventually he considers the natures of other persons and comes to speak of evidence grounded in the generality of human nature. The grounds and the pattern of response to the grounds remain consistent; the evidence gives every appearance of being in the first instance a descriptive psychology. So it is not accidental that the primary half of a comprehensive work on the nature and destiny of man should involve a study of human nature.

The secular existentialist forms his position similarly. While Sartre's novels and philosophic ideas may or may not be of interest in themselves the descriptive psychology presented in his work is penetrating enough to merit careful study in its own right. Descriptive material of this type may certainly be advanced to document what for the existentialist has to be the primary metaphysical problem: what is the reality of first existence? That this turns out to be a descriptive psychology, assertive rather than derivative, should not occasion any surprise. The existentialist must make a beginning somewhere. His effort to describe something comes perilously close to implying substance; indeed, he may escape it only because it is the cultural habit of the psychologist not to be concerned with the substantial. Psychologists have trained their publics to refrain from asking them the metaphysical question; insofar as the existentialist is a psychologist he may be suffered to escape embarrassment by adopting the latter's protective coloration. People tend to think that students of human nature know something, or know something new or something different; so they are nice to them and let them alone. When the metaphysical question is finally put the existentialist position may turn out to be simply a temporary nexus of cerebral custom which, when questioned, vanishes and leaves the question standing in its stead.

Reflective positions must always define the nature of individual man. A good many kinds of philosophic stance begin with observations on human nature; that this is so may be a matter of temperament or of procedural convenience. It is not inevitably the first concern, however, for views of human nature can be derived from other principles. It may be useful at this point to set the existential reference over against a rationalistic reference for what the comparison may show about the nature of thought as relation of subject and object.

Reason As Conceptual Instrument

The view of reason presented here assumes a number of relations referred to in companion papers. Knowing is understood to be of a single order of relation for different fields and to be operational in character. It is understood to be conceptual in the broadest and most comprehensive sense, active, grasping, definitive, establishing a fundamental connection between the substantive self and the phases of the real which can respond to the approach of reason. As each of the faculties of the self can be thought of as comprising a one-to-one relation with correspondences outside the self, so reason can be understood in this way; its function is to be the initial and unifying relation of the rational self and its rational environment.

The ground-notion on which this view of reason is founded, that of the nature of knowing as conceptual, is indeed heavily rational. This is to say that conceptual knowing, fundamental to every kind of awareness, assumes the existence of idea as real, and requires that world-view, or the stance of knowing, so to speak, be also understood as determinative in the selection of phases of the real which actually make up the Janus-relation of definition and discovery. What is involved here is the notion of the self as lens, through the assertive refraction of which the world which the self comes to know is brought forward from the chaos of unlimited possibility.

The pivot-points in a variety of fundamental formulations of the real control regions of concern which tend to overlap, and this characteristic obtains generally in reflective formulations. The immediate effect is that reason as conceived here tends to subsume elements of the real which would also be pre-empted by existential, empiricist, or other points of view. The tendency of reflective world-views to gobble up large parts of each other's territories must always be borne in mind.

Notice in this view that reason as conceptual instrument has enormously greater grasp and deeper metaphysical reality than has reason conceived of as simply the periodic rationalizing of data, a function of which is ordinarily a segment in the empirical process of scientific knowing. The metaphysical decision which is inevitably made prior to the taking of a position in epistemology is different in these two conceptions of reason. The latter regards reason as a tool in the proper management of data empirically registered. The former posits reason as instrument of mind in the prehension of rational reality. It has been sufficiently indicated that the range of concern in the former instance is also vastly greater and not subject to restriction by empirical method or by baseless ascription of independent reality to external objects.

And yet these are essentially identical reasons for reason does serve to manage data as well as to establish fundamental relations of subject and object. The difference stems from the prior metaphysical decision, as is generally the case. The implied position might then be a straight

Platonic rationalism, a Platonic realism in Mr. Wild's sense, or an Aristotelian realism, except that the Aristotelian universal is rather too local and contrived an affair; it might be a Whiteheadian rationalism or realism except again that total substitution of process for substance suggests only a passing phase in the unending drive to make viable the relation of the self and its setting.

The Morphology of Thought as Cultural Motion

Instead of supposing that the truth is wholly encompassed in each successive philosophic system or for that matter in the general positions casually held by public groups perhaps what is most needed is the willingness to ascertain which aspects of the truth are being hunted for in which periods and which cultural settings, and for which purposes. Thought may be different things in different periods and may be operationally and functionally related to different facets of the real. Thus an empiricist age may be culturally justified first as compensation for a previous period of rational formulation which has grown old and needs revision, and then as a means of introducing new phases of reality in order to raise the index of complexity and so to make available new ranges of data and new dimensions of awareness. The error will come in supposing that an empiricist period is better justified than its predecessors, for it is not, except that it is chronologically later, has the advantage of additional perspective, and serves a purpose different in direction from those of its forerunners; each of these exceptions will apply as accurately to its successors. A viewpoint can be said to serve a social end in that it adds to the dimension of the known, but this would not be the end of the matter, for social valuation is not fundamental. Strictly social reference-points in morality and metaphysics are on a par with alleged "flat places in the carburetor," those quaint booby-traps of automotive medicine.

Similarly, existentialist re-assessments of human nature and human existence may respond to the cultural needs of a particular period. Existentialism is perhaps more than ordinarily a cultural reflection, certainly more the child of its time than is a definitive rationalism; it is also not quite competent philosophically, and this is some slight disadvantage in the idea-marts of the time. By definition it cannot answer philosophic inquiries in the terms in which the inquiries are put unless it wishes to risk becoming something other than it says it is. In consequence it may be reduced to making its responses in grunts.

For the moment the appeal of existentialism is not impaired by its philosophic vagueness, for contextual reasons, partly the result of its stance and rootage and partly the effect of its heavily emotional component. The current interest in existentialism, already reported to be waning, may reflect the inward-turning of the age, its psychologism, its devotion to analysis of the self, its placing of personality and the western psychological tradition at the heart of its positive position.

It is a strange phenomenon to observe, for this youthful time likes to think of itself as earthy, sensible, rooted in fact, divesting itself of religious frills and frippery, bearing straight down on the hard-boiled world. The contradiction between scientific or empiricist awareness and the emotional fundaments of existentialist awareness are lost on the younger existentialist of today. He is likely either to accept it imperturbably or simply to disregard it. His attention is elsewhere, on the emotional reality of his nature and on the values he ascribes to its objective reference-points, to reality emotionally prehended.

The cultural compensation is readily discernible. The tendency of scientific thought in the space age to go out of focus for the non-scientist may be having its inevitable effect. Other streams of thought are convenient to hand, one of the nearest being that which derives from western psychology. The bewildered mind withdraws its interest from the mode of confusion and re-aligns itself among familiar surroundings. It could be expected that the modern student of humanities should find refuge in the certainties of the self. It is after all what follows him around most closely most of the time.

It is difficult to suppose that the form and structure of thought in any period are not in part responsive to the cultural condition of the time even while metaphysically a constituent of it. This is not to say that the morphology of thought is culturally determined, for culture may better be determined by the nature of thought. The multi-faceted potentiality of thought may indeed be thrown into relief this way or that by assumptions and proclivities of an age, but the nature of thought must be said to be determined by its own potentialities, and on the same ultimate ground as the rest of the created universe. In large reference, then, the appearance of an existential emphasis in assertive fields represents a resurgent alternation of reflective concern rooted in the conceptual nature of knowing and responsive to cultural history, the contemporary phase of which follows a rational or realistic episode and will in turn be followed by other rational or realist episodes reformulated in varied ways.

Existentialism is therefore one of a number of philosophical interstices, each phase obtaining for a time between periods of more precise formulation and serving utilitarian as well as intrinsic ends. It cannot be expected to cover much ground in its recurrent phases; its ranges of data do not extend far beyond the implications of psychology as a region of study. The remainder of nature and the settings of life are present in it only by implication and are not really taken into account. This judgment bears less on Thomistic existentialism which is a theme of religious realism and is not required to develop its independent metaphysic and theory of knowledge.

Major modes of thought should be expected to succeed each other, although not in regular or equalized orders and certainly not in readily predictable forms. Among these successive stages in the matrix of reflection the emphasis on priority of existence as fundamental datum should re-appear now and again, as a comet may circle into view in the sky every few hundred years. It cannot be expected to provide philosophic erudition; most existentialisms refrain from this by agreement, and if occasionally one of its representations does become philosophically explicit by that very effort it presumably transmutes itself into something else. It can be expected to add to the raw materials from which philosophies are constructed, or at least to remind philosophers of the realities of personal existence which they are apt to forget as they weave their abstract patterns.

It may not seem to matter that the schools and systems of thought succeed each other in these ways. After all, their own potentialities are served, and the potentialities of intellect are served, in their earnest succession one of the other. Ignorance of the larger view may even be a guarantee of the greatest possible intrinsic effectiveness of each viewpoint, since every philosopher feels he has at last discovered the truth and behaves accordingly. The value of the greater perspective, throwing the sub-phases into relief, is of course that the prior metaphysical decision and the conception of the ultimate will be more competent. The truth will not be more accurately known in any final way, but its immensity may better lend its shadows to the reaches of the mind.

V Education Is One

It is curious how often in western thought a major and a minor strand run parallel courses for a time, addressing themselves to a common problem, and permitting by a difference of approach the inference of divergent views of what is real. Frequently the inference is merely apparent, and elements held in common reduce the divergence to one of form.

Education in America has been divided into the so-called conventional and progressive schools of thought. The division may have had its uses; it has certainly had its irritations. From a practical rather than a philosophic standpoint, and having reference mainly to higher education, it may be useful to reconsider the validity of the dualism.

Conventional Education's View of Itself

Conventional education sees itself in part as the vehicle by which the great cultural resources of the past are preserved and made available to later times. Cultural resources consist of the records of human insights and expressions in divers media, reflections of the concerns of men and of their creative responses to those concerns. The emphasis falls upon the enduring human characteristics and their products which recur in succeeding ages. The work of colleges and universities is in part to preserve these records and to present them in renascent forms to the changing generations of students. Cultural memory exists in tension between the mind and books. It is constantly revised and re-created through study; its meanings contribute to understanding of the present and to the endless endeavor to grasp the significance of life.

Further, conventional education provides for the preservation and extension of knowledge concerning the nature of things. Scientific resources consist of recorded concepts and theories, investigative results constantly revised and rethought, and the methods and facilities by which they are achieved. Science exists in tension between the mind of the scientist and the subject of his study, having major reference to the ways in which he works.

The faculty in a conventional educational institution serves several functions. Original research, the discovery or rethinking of aspects of the past or present, is a necessity in some form for a teacher in the intellectual fields. Human nature needs to create; each person should make a distinctive contribution to the general development even though it may be but a small part of a large and intricate project. Original study in subject matter or in the art of teaching provokes the teaching mind to living effort and at the same time allows the learning mind to benefit from residence on the active frontiers of knowledge.

Conventional teaching or organized around significant foci within the cultural and natural disciplines, emphasizing in recent years the consideration of problems rather than simple conveyance of material or chronological surveys. The standard lecture, a method widely used in large classes, is in its effective form a means of throwing into juxtaposition arrays of facts and ideas such that the listeners experience the challenge of new perspectives and unresolved problems. Doors snap open, so to speak, up and down a long corridor.

The conventional student enters an established system of research and teaching classes and selects the sequences which meet his interests. He may cross lines within the system if he will exert the necessary force. Study is properly a form of creation; perception is followed by integration and response; originality is a characteristic of the encounter of mind and idea.

Progressive Education's View of Conventional Education

According to progressive critics, conventional education is a deadening repetition of facts and theories, insistent predilections of the teacher recounted in dull ways and periodically required again in examinations. Subject-centered study is a device of self-indulgent professors to discourage change so that students will want to hear what the teacher wants to say.

Since ordinary faculties are promoted on the basis of written produce they must spend their time on the editing and writing of books. Students are a necessary evil in an otherwise happy life. The system centers upon preoccupied teachers to whom subjects are more important than people. The conventional professor proceeds methodically to his appointed classroom, presumably wearing red underwear and regarding the world with a glassy stare, and there deposits little rabbity pellets of used knowledge which are supposed to ferment or blow up or otherwise accomplish something while the learned pedant departs to resume digestion. One is reminded of the Virgil Partch cartoon of several years ago in which an army sergeant lams down the center aisle of a lecture room followed by the placid stares of a platoon of pouting woodenheads, leaving on the desk a little oval object and a pin: ''And that, Gentlemen,'' calls the running rube, ''is the way you pull the pin on a hand grenade.''

Some progressive educators believe that the conflict between the scholarly and teaching functions in conventional faculties could be resolved by a division of personnel. Some should be scholars and some should be teachers, but few should be both. Any claim to good teaching in conventional institutions is ordinarily denied by definition; professors of subject-matter accomplish genuine teaching only accidentally if at all.

The victim of the conventional system, says progressive education, is the featherhead who succumbs to pressure for the accepted educational commodity and spends four stultified years dragging in and out of huge lecture halls, wasting his intellectual substance in brain-beating and wild parties.

Progressive Education's View of Itself

Progressive education views itself as the sole educational process by which responsible individuals are created out of the debris left by their families and their social groups. A philosophy of development is implied in this. The parent is the enemy of the child as the cultural past is the enemy of the present. A break between them is inevitable, taking the form of revolt against familial and social tradition, a disintegration of ideas and behavior followed by reintegration of ideas and conduct on a reasoned, individual base.

The diamond on which the wheel spins in this educational theory lies precisely here. Other aspects of the educative process radiate from this hard point. The individual personality of the student stands irreducibly at the center of the progressive system. All else is geared to its needs. If in the conventional system the student is sacrificed to the faculty, in the progressive system the faculty is sacrificed to the student. Youth is king—as long as he is reasonably polite.

As the student is an end in himself he is philosophically alone even while immersed by intention in the social group. Communication between faculty and student exists in profusion but is restricted in kind. One person's perceptions and processes can never be really understood by another. The educational institution does not know what a study means to a student or what he learns or thinks. A college is a place where young people develop; its job is to provide the best conditions for learning. But it does not know what learning is in any instance, and it must therefore reserve judgment on the student's work. It should excise officious administration and directive teaching in order to let learning happen.

The student's function is to grow. Growth, a precious concept, refers to the development of life processes and the realization of positive potentials which, though difficult to describe except in terms of an individual case, are nevertheless very important.

The faculty must challenge the student, help him to develop his interests, and somehow, in the midst of concentric and exclusive worlds, motivate him to work to the limit of his capacity. Research on the faculty level is unimportant. Even research in education is not central, since the knowledge necessary for ideal operation of the progressive system is held to be already available. The work of the faculty is to preside over the rebirth of human beings, a process the conditions of which are certain but the essence of which is mystery.

The cultural stream of tradition, central in conventional education, is absent here. It is as if the cosmos were constantly re-created in the successive perceptions of each new mind. The march of history is a myth. The perceiving mind provides the only synthesis of cultural materials. The individual personality is a ganglion the lines of which reach to all reality; organization of knowledge is possible only in terms of its conceptions, partial or comprehensive.

Conventional Education's View of Progressive Education

According to conventional critics, progressive education dwells in a house of mirrors. Solid learning does not take place within it; there is no reliable acquaintance with the vast stream of natural and human history, and no discipline to develop the acquaintance. The student contemplates his growth, watches his wonderful parts unfolding, busily satisfies his needs, and enjoys experiencing experience. He is a divinity with many arms, preoccupied with self, posturing, brooding upon his problems, entangled in a web of his own spinning. When he has free time he sees his psychiatrist, since all students in progressive institutions are emotionally disturbed; that is why they are in progressive institutions. After several years of this they presumably become fine people, but they do not know anything and they are not competent to do anything. They are mature fruits; they just revolve and shine.

As the chief function of the student is to grow, the chief function of the faculty is to let the student grow. Growing is becoming more of what one is already. While progressive education feels that it provides a learning environment which causes students to react selectively, in socially useful ways as well as in accordance with individual potential, conventional education sees the vine running wild over the landscape, unpruned and undirected, wasting its energy in growth for its own sake and to no useful purpose.

The role of a small-boned faculty is seen as essentially obstetrical—the perpetration of a monstrous midwifery where the adult contingent stands by with bowls of hot water and towels and bloody hands, assisting in the birth, sheltering the blundering infant, sympathizing and empathizing with its transgressions, until out of the welter of trial and error alabaster youth steps forth reborn, become at last the responsible being which the evil ingredients of his composition and his past had heretofore forbidden. In the depths of personality is an individual essence never realized except through the process of salvation as prescribed by progressive education. Like all religious systems still in an early stage of development, progressive education is based on faith and establishes an elect redeemed from ruin through a particular procedure.

The pivotal faith in human nature applies only to the young in age. Teaching personnel, being subject to the automatic corruption of the adult world, cannot be trusted. They must be constantly cut back, held within bonds, lest the fatal push toward officialdom and bureaucracy repress the tender, growing shoots.

A progressive educator, according to conventional judgment, deteriorates in his personal organization as times goes on. The teaching situation turns him from concentration upon a productive field of interest to preoccupation with the psychology of student personality. The labors of instructing and learning are avoided; classes receive less and less preparation. There is little opportunity for study; course material is repeated year after year. Time passes in reflection upon the private lives of students; direct involvement with students increases without providing objective leadership. The progressive teacher becomes a secular confessor with a beginner's knowledge of Freud. He loses touch with his academic profession and grows old congratulating himself on his unique value to the young.

Education Is One

The aim of education is to stir the young in constructive ways, through learning of things and ideas and learning with respect to self. All possible systems of education entail this aim. All possible systems depend on the inspiration of the great teacher for definition of ideals of accomplishment for teachers and students alike. Conflicting viewpoints may in time resolve their differences and reach a middle ground, but the process is long and disputatious. If the conventional and progressive positions can be seen to hold certain elements in common the implications of the recurrence may be of interest.

Theories of culture and personal growth aside, the bare bones of education in any system may be observed to consist of teacher, student and subject, each with appropriate functions and requirements. The teacher leads in plan and implementation. He imparts and questions, now more, now less, in varying combinations. The student receives and responds with a counter-contribution which may be verbal or silent. The teaching problem is that of obtaining the largest possible response from the student in the subject concerned—the excitement so genuine that its direction is part of its genius.

Progressive education substitutes the personal challenge of the student by the teacher for the conventional challenge by examination. The element of challenge must be present. Without it the conventional course produces merely regurgitation, and the progressive classroom produces idleness. Discipline also is indispensable. Where the system does not compel labor through the threat of examination the teacher must go into the classroom situation with great personal force, requiring accomplishment by direct establishment of standards. Contrary to folklore, students left to themselves do not necessarily grow, and hurdles alone do not induce the conquering leap.

Observation suggests that conventional and progressive education alike use force. If education takes place the student is challenged and responds creatively. The mechanisms of challenge may vary but the function is common.

Leadership cannot be eliminated in education. Conventional education has been pictured as stifling student originality through dictatorial repression, while progressive education is believed to authorize its students to run loose without supervision in the interest of encouraging adolescent growth. Neither description is accurate. Observation indicates that genuine leadership is part of teaching, providing constructive adult example and advice as frames of reference for student participation and gradual assumption of responsibility. Without reference frames the student is subject to confusion. Leadership may be overplayed or underplayed, but where education of any kind is successful it is present in effective forms.

Judgment of students is mistakenly called into question. Conventional education is said to judge students by mark-levels which through usage become ends in themselves. Progressive education may use a variant marking system or may depend on written evaluations. Judgment is, however, always present although it may be blurred in its precision of application and may be applied in different ways. Only a procedural difference separates the written examination and the face-to-face canvass of the student's knowledge of course material.

It seems misleading to ascribe to conventional and progressive education divergent views of human nature when the creative effort of both systems is directed to the same end. Their intentions are largely the same and their methods involve the stuff of human nature and its potential development. There are differences of emphasis between the systems reflecting the interests of the educators. Yet insofar as institutions of either type are successful they depend for their success upon their realization of a process the structure of which they hold in common.

Normally, the old teach the young that which age and experience have taught them; learning may be described in personal terms as the response of the young to the old. Progressive education, retaining the adult as teacher for the sake of expediency, de-emphasizes age and bows endlessly to youth. The student or learning group is seen as the elect, while the rest of humanity, trusted only in abstract democratic theory, is seen as corrupted by the evil of adulthood. Yet this aberration does not contravene the pattern since it is a by-product of concern for those who learn. Progressive education is fascinated by the process of encouraging the young at particular age-levels to live through their revolts. One might study the effects of the alliance of progressive education with Freudian psychology in the 1920's, and the effects upon education of the development of Freudian psychology away from that alliance in the last twenty years.

For conventional education human nature is creative and responsive; it achieves responsibility by re-creating what it receives. Education presents conceptions, evidence and experience for what validity they may have and what re-formation they enable. Conventional education believes that past experience can suggest answers to present questions, and does not hesitate to direct study to this end while it realizes that the answers and the questions will be altered in the re-creation.

Progressive education describes human nature in these same terms, but it is also, within certain age-limits, sanctified in a special way. Education then becomes a hallowed procedure in which the adult world, itself leprous and unclean, is permitted to minister to the needs of the student world like the sinner before the Grail. The vision will vanish in time, only to be re-created in the next student generation. The process of education is of exclusive interest.

Conventional education appears to function so that a major product of its operations will be cultural continuity. This has obvious values, and in the present view provides the stuff of history and social process. Progressive education modifies the common concepts and procedures to bear down on difference.

It further appears that progressive education basically does what conventional education does, and that it must do so if it is to provide education at all. When progressive education diverges from conventional practice it does so simply in order to be different, to break stereotypic adhesions, to force teachers and students to rethink methods and theories. There are acknowledged values in reformulating old theories and in being compelled to achieve educational ends by procedures just noticeably different from the usual. These values need not persuade us, however, that the differences which progressive education introduces alter the nature of education or the requirements made of it if it is to be effective. Similarly, the view of human nature is mainly the same. One may scowl at conventional education because it looks over the head of the individual to gaze at mountains far away. One may scoff at progressive education because it plows the furrow with head descended, nuzzling the near-by earth, its horizon the waving grasses. Visions have come from mountains, and sermons have been found in stones.

For all that there is much in common the flinty partisans may not wish to discontinue the pleasures of conflict and self-justification. Conventional education will roll its eyes and cluck its tongues at the sins of the beardless prophets. Progressive education will huff and puff at the stupid ancients whose minds were snagged in the Middle Ages. Tension among points of view may be an ordinary condition of group thinking by which the myopia of the single mind is corrected through the perspectives of other minds.

Yet how enticing the speculation on gain in work accomplished, from whatever standpoint, if virtuous whines were replaced by toleration and respect. The several schools might teach, and students learn, in better heart.

VI Conjunction Over Harvard

A discussion some years ago of the Harvard Memorial Church, settled thereafter by a sensible decision of the University, may have been a local aspect of some immensely interesting philosophic changes of a broad nature—changes which have considerable significance elsewhere as well as for participants in the exchanges at Harvard.

The issue from the first had general as well as particular implications. An enterprising graduate student questioned whether the many-faceted modern university should commit itself to a single religious position in any of its common parts. When a community of scholars must necessarily represent a multiplicity of viewpoints, should the University Church be defined in terms of a single major position? Definition of the Memorial Church as a Christian institution had tended to exclude non-Christian occasional services. Did such a definition also have implications for the holding of other major viewpoints throughout the University?

So far as the Memorial Church was concerned, the University commented that it had always been within the Christian tradition, and that, in consequence, services within it were normally presided over by clergymen of some Christian connection. Nevertheless, in view of the complex nature of the Harvard population of today, the University decided that non-Christian occasional services could be conducted independently in the Memorial Church so long as all concerned thought it appropriate.

In its local aspect this was not a large matter. The Memorial Church would surely have been defined as broadly Christian. There would not have been much else to call it, unless it were to be described as some sort of noble barn, architecturally distinguished but religiously uncommitted. Many churches would consider themselves in a predicament if such an alternative were widely adopted. A question inevitably arose over the advisability of strict application of the definition. The reply of the University meant that a genuinely religious occasional service, of whatever origin, would not detract from the accepted dedication of the Memorial Church to Christian uses.

Restraint of this kind in the application of large principles may be all-important for ecumenical problems generally, where hard-and-fast doctrinal interpretations retard unification but where the experiential commonalities draw together people of diverse religious connections. The late Dean Willard Sperry used to say that theological differences tended to keep religious leaders divided, whereas the common experience of worship tended to draw those same leaders together.

But what of the interesting background of this matter—those far-reaching changes in the realm of ideas which are reflected in local issues from time to time? To begin with, let it be observed that changes in the realm of ideas are seldom very large. Supposedly contradictory points of view often have broad areas of agreement, and not infrequently have common historical origins such that they may sometimes be considered as technically in schism, one from the other. Similarly, the mood which marks an intellectual age often retains major characteristics of a preceding period which it supposedly destroyed, but which in actuality it preserved in altered form.

In the Harvard of the 'fifties there had been a change—a very small one in the total scheme of things, but enough to produce a slight movement among the centers of gravity which characterize a university. The Divinity School, emerging from a quietly brilliant period in which, through a distinguished and memorable faculty, it reflected with remarkable accuracy the finest ideals of the University, entered upon a slightly different and more assertive phase marked, perhaps, by a higher concentration of ideas around traditional Christian centers. This new phase has promise of its own, especially in the comprehensive way in which it is developing. And, in addition, it represents in some measure the tendencies of the time.

It seems clear that the major fields of investigative and intellectual inquiry are moving toward larger conceptual formulations, and that this tide is running with great strength in the present period. The natural and social sciences show this tendency as well as the several philosophic and religious fields. Not all divisions of any field, but some divisions of all fields, show it—those sections concerned with synthesis and comprehensive formulation as distinct from analytic preoccupations.

The movement of the Divinity School into an assertive phase is in one sense a specification of a concern which has been central with the School since its founding, as indeed it must have been and must always be with any Protestant or Catholic theological institution. In another sense, it serves as a movement toward a comprehensive conception of reality in terms of which the problems of the twentieth century can be understood. In a peculiarly demanding way, the call for a transcending arch of ideas is being sounded on all sides. The vacuity of life without generalized meanings has issued its promissory notes redeemable on demand, and when the orders of events have run their courses for a time, for long enough to show what fruits they can produce, the notes are abruptly summoned for redemption. This is now happening in many phases of American life.

It makes no difference whether we approve of this or not. It is taking place regardless of our feelings. We must make our peace with it—classicists, humanists, scientists, liberals, traditionalists in any sense—for it is one of the great facts of our time. That this is so, raises special tensions within a college or university, where the fields are staffed with men dedicated to study and investigation in accordance with a diversity of comprehensive concepts. This, too, is one of the great facts of our time. Nothing can or should be done about this in an overt or administrative way. The many fields of endeavor, each responding to its own conceptions, each represented by men of the highest caliber, each with its own contributions to make, must simply learn to live with one another in the slightly altered configuration which the renewed emphasis on Christianity makes inevitable. Perhaps it may help a little to be aware of the movements underlying particular manifestations, and through understanding to be prepared for individual issues like that of the Memorial Church which may appear from the shift in the weighted pattern of university relationships.

In a sense, these movements of the centers of gravity within the "community of memory and hope" are indeed very slight, and in the total scheme of things the resultant changes are also slight. In another sense, it is all rather like some grand conjunction in the skies, where diverse entities, seemingly unrelated, suddenly appear in close and unfamiliar context, forming a new pattern which alters the configuration of the heavens for a time and startles the placid watcher with strange perspectives.

The extent of substantial interaction among religious and humanistic fields is difficult to determine, and may be quite impossible to gauge. The relationship is, at least, a deep and complex one. It has been remarked that the climate of an age may be closely related to the climates of ages preceding and following, related historically by retention and transformation of common elements, and related transversely through similarity or near-identity of function and procedure. With respect to the brooding political conflict of our time, some have pointed out the likelihood that philosophic and political forms of Marxist thought represent, historically and typically, schismatic forms of Christian thought. The implication of this possibility for the necessary development of mutual understanding of rival societies may bear reflection.

With respect to the major ideological conjunction of our age, the relation between religious and scientific fields of thought, still more interesting implications can be had for the taking. Some have pointed out that the recent intellectual climate, commonly considered a scientific period, derives historically from the Middle Ages and preserves the faiths of that supposedly vanished time. Even while we stand on the threshold of the age of space and electronics, of human mastery over nature to degrees undreamed of—no sparkling anticipation of which need be questioned in the slightest—some assert that, in a fundamental epistemological sense, the age of science separately conceived, defined as a line of thought and study different in kind from religious or other lines of Western thought, is already dead; that the age of science in any unique sense no longer exists but must be considered to have rejoined the main stream of the Western tradition—with what conceptual and procedural consequences who can foretell?

Any one of a hundred pivot points might mark the replacement of the so-called scientific age with an age of common thought. To humor the weird whimsy which sometimes appears in the history of ideas, let us choose as the point of passage the publication of Mr. Conant's Bampton Lectures in 1952, in which he noted that the natural sciences do not have a separate or different means to knowledge but rather depend on a conceptual epistemology as do other fields of study. With his customary candor he observed that this description of scientific epistemology represented a revision of his earlier view of the matter. It will not do to blame Mr. Conant for the uses to which we put his insights; he is more than welcome to recoil in horror if he likes. One may properly record, however, that the establishment of a common epistemology among the natural sciences and religions of the West (and of the East) has implications of immense significance for religious and scientific studies. The present age may well be on the verge of stupendous and unpredictable change. We may note, with perhaps a pardonable glint of mischief, that the signal service to religion in modern times may have been rendered by none other than James B. Conant.

All this is to say that the recent emergence of specifically Christian emphases in religious interest and study at Harvard and the repercussions which this must have in the relations of the Divinity School and the University constitute a highly complex succession of adjustments the secondary waves of which have not yet begun to be felt. Assessment could come too soon. The conjunction must be lived with to be understood.

One final caution must be borne in mind. An appalling penalty obtains with every major concept in religious or secular thought. Any formulation may endure for a greater or a lesser time, but by its very existence it is sentenced to eventual destruction. Humanistic and religious scholars, natural scientists, students in all fields, may be well used to this and to the pain of relinquishing one pattern of understanding in behalf of another. No field is immune to this form of death and transfiguration. Philosophies and concepts of nature disappear and are replaced by others. Formulations of reality in Christian terms are also constantly split asunder to be succeeded by reformulations in larger, if still Christian, terms.

There remains for purposes of reflection and comtemplation the curious witness of history that the meanings of existence, at best obscure, can still be understood most commonly in terms of personal drama. What is to become of this witness no one can say. That it must be a factor in contemplative studies within the foreseeable future, no one can doubt.

VII American Education as Metaphysics: The Religious Consequence

Every civilization can be interpreted as an enormous adventure in understanding. It consists of a complex of idea-systems and associated patterns of activity organized toward self-expression. This is to say, a culture lives out its life testing a system of values, a value being simply a relation between idea and act sustained by individuals capable of rational judgment. A civilization may be said to flourish when it cares most and does most about its central concerns; it declines when it cares less and does less about them.

A far greater range of thought-and-action systems could certainly come into being than have so far been tried out on this planet. The profound differences among religions of East and West, their differing reflections of human nature, their ideas of the ultimate, and their descriptions of the universe, as well as the extraordinary futuristic implications of Western conceptual thought in the present day, all suggest that the notion of relativity or multiplicity of foci ought to be applied to the category of world-views instead of being confined within one supposedly modern scientific world-picture. Substantial intimations of Divinity are not affected by relativity attachable to world-views. What is under study is the variety of efforts of the human mind to grasp the nature and setting of existence.

Elsewhere it has been sufficiently understood that the psychologies and cosmologies which become the building-stones of world-views are heavily projective in character and are only momentarily if at all receptual. If the conceptions of things are in part constructed of man's nature and interests and in part from selected facets of his environment there must be some accuracy in every tested formulation of the nature of things. Every reflective tradition must have its truth, though it may also have its error or distortion.

Metaphysical relations ought perhaps to be considered in actual instances, and in fact the present sketch derives from the New England town meeting and from the profound concern of villagers and townsmen for local issues in education. Any actual instance, however, has its metaphysical connections. The individual or event is the rooted manifestation of an idea, a general idea which exists in its own realm and eventuates as it will or as best it can. It is entirely practical to move back and forth between a generality and its particular, and with this acknowledgment the general idea is the better described.

Grant that this description of human nature runs counter to predominant views of the 20th century. After all, American society has been running about for some seventy years now with its metaphysical conceptions in a decapitated condition, ever since the casual scimitar of William James whistled through the gentle airs at Harvard and set the heads of generalities to tumbling in all directions. James was interested in particulars; he wanted to pick them up one or two at a time, turn them around and around and look at them and keep them separated from their heads. Since James' time because of the unexpected availability of very large numbers of particulars it has become fashionable to occupy oneself with data immediately underfoot. Gradually the Western world has moved over into a veritable universe of particulars. General ideas have tended to reduce to verbal connections between separate facts, the effect being to limit sharply the interpretive significance of human life. Reflective meaning has become the casualty of preoccupation with small detail.

There is good reason for this. When a world-view or any comprehensive theoretical construct of lesser but still large dimensions is in process of change it is normal for the energy of its time to be largely withdrawn from its theoretical reach and to be concentrated among its numerous particulars. The scope of attention being limited it tends to be applied to the welter of particulars in the foreground of whatever perspective is available. After a while the natural balance of the self records the conceptual imbalance and the distortion is redressed in the direction of the general idea.

The cultural adventure of American life, whatever else it may also have been, has seemed to fall in an activous realm. It is as if the metaphysical forms associated with stratified societies of the old world had been conceived too firmly. When transplanted to open country in the new world where the physical frontier was constantly receding philosophic concern turned away from the general idea and became heavily over-balanced toward the particular object. Stubbing its toe, so to speak, on the rugged coastline of New England the dominant metaphysics of an epoch fell flat on its face across the entire continent of North America and ended by staring at the floor of the Pacific Ocean.

The effect has been a miasmic preoccupation with things, data, objects, materialities, as distinct from generalities. To a degree American "individualism" is no doubt articulated with this longstanding immersion in particulars. A large part of contemporary life consists of getting things done rather than of thinking about them in any fundamental way. It is not only that pure contemplation is often neglected; practical uses of generality are also neglected. Business and industrial firms overlook the uses of reflection on even those general ideas immediately relevant to their material production. A straight empirical approach by itself is insufficient for the resolution of highly technical questions in manufacturing. There ought to be a willingness to consider the general ideas which control particular ranges of empirical data in order to develop efficient ways of handling related ranges of data. General ideas for industrial or business purposes, as for example in the making of paper on the Fourdrinier machine, are restricted in scope by the requirement of close articulation with the task; they are usually not generalities of the largest dimensions. Yet without them questions in industrial technology often are resolved if at all only by accident or by trial and error, an expensive procedure in machine and personnel time.

Education is not an exception to the American emphasis on the activous nature of life. Ordinary people are constantly becoming excited about local issues in education, and are constantly roaring their motors into the midst of the fray. Citizens in small communities want to decide personally whether to close Shady Glen grade school, how much to pay Mrs. Elton Smith who teaches French in the town high school and doubles as principal, and whether to run a bus for children who live more than a mile and a half from the Center school. Education budgets are fought over with all degrees of personal commitment, close attention being given to each financial issue. The articulation of school with home and family, a mutual reliance the fundamental nature of which is merely obscured rather than altered by the remoteness and large size of city schools, points to a significant dimension of reality in the American mind.

It is not too much to say that in education the American lay philosopher, the citizen who may earn his living in any one of a thousand different ways, gives evidence of his fundamental beliefs. Here very often is that which is most important to him. The reason is simple enough: immediately beneath the surface of educational policy is the powerful conception held by the community on the nature of man and the ideal society. In the play of issues in and around education in the small community the drama of individual commitment in the moral realm is made clear.

Without a profound metaphysical grounding the activous American concern for education makes no sense at all. On whatever side of whatever educational issues particular anxieties may fall the conclusion has to be the same. In attitudes toward education of children and young people a rough-and-ready, supposedly anti-intellectual people discloses the depth of its metaphysic and its religion.

American life has been said to be an enormous adventure in understanding. So far as ready observation runs, it has tended to involve itself with things, with nature and with natural objects. It has turned from the realm of ideas, and not infrequently it has fought shy in its public life of the man whose primary concern is ideas. Existence must however involve the general idea in its own right and as ground for the existence of particulars. So there has to have been a mistake somewhere. Civilizations can make errors, as individual persons can; indeed, such errors may be useful excursions into practical expression of metaphysical possibility, adding thereby to the world's awareness of what it can and ought—or ought not—to do. But in the scouring of energy poured into American educational problems the secret of the matter stands revealed. Here American society acknowledges that it is philosophically and metaphysically alive, that it is really neither anti-intellectual nor just rough-and-ready. It is on the contrary deeply involved with the meanings of human life. Whether from cultural habit or from embarrassment, or as a consequence of its adventuring into empirical ways of knowing, it is reluctant to voice its reflective concerns as such; it prefers to express itself through educational policy and practice.

No object or event can be free of its general idea. A local address to a point in town meeting, a court judgment, any expressions of actual or potential policy, have in common the characteristic of direct relation to general principles of which the local instances are projective representations. The degrees of emotional involvement in education go to confirm the real depth of metaphysical concern.

A philosophy of education has as one of its major components a philosophy of human nature. Its educational bent will follow the bent of its reflective psychology. Is man a classic spirit inheriting the breaths of former times? Then the schools of today will be formed accordingly, to teach what former times have known. Is he rather a spirit above the limits of time, bespeaking with his lesser instruments the universe of heart and mind? Then the schools will be formed accordingly, making the necessary assertions on the realities and ways of knowing. Is man an animal, inheritor of a biological past, whose ideals are deceptive accidents in the flowing of his hormones? Then the schools will be formed accordingly, perhaps with special attention to physiological chemistry. Or is man a walking echo of other men, bouncing off his fellow humans, picking up spots and slivers of reality, creating an amalgam of the pseudo-real from a wide array of nasal noise? Then the schools will be formed accordingly, their stock-in-trade the skills of communication.

Philosophies of education have other large components—epistemologies, philosophies of nature, and occasionally philosophies of the objective apart from nature. Points of departure are functions of interest and are grounded in temperament. The system must stand the tests; that is the important thing. A point of departure in a system may be only a matter of biographical curiosity.

It is difficult not to conclude that the conception of education as the reality-dimension in which American society expresses its metaphysical concerns, whether or not it troubles to acknowledge this fact to itself, leads inevitably into the contemporary tangle of religion and education. Religion can be described as the expression of a metaphysics with which it is directly articulated. In large perspective it is unnecessary to distinguish between the two. Metaphysics then comprises the systemic fundaments obtaining at the roots of every intellective position, explicit or implicit. It makes the statements concerning the grounds of things required by any position, immediate or remote, involving either generalities or particulars. It is the most abstract of possible dimensions or levels of comprehension. Deriving from it and bridging the way from generality to particularity is the religious dimension, partly metaphysical, partly general, partly expressional, ceremonial, and social, and partly particularistic.

Religion is predominantly a universal dimension, the characteristics of which are to be perceived in every realm of human interest and commitment—provided the personal involvement is sufficient. Certain atypical assumptions are built into this view. Religion is universal in a generic sense, confined to no particularist or historical tradition, not exclusively Christian, Islamic, Judaic, Buddhist, or other; it is as readily secularist or classically anti-'religious' as it is formally or traditionally 'religious'; it can be positivistic, scientistic, purely social, even political. Definition of a position as religious is in some part by recognition of far-reaching emotional or attitudinal commitment of persons to it, by acknowledgment that it serves to focus for its holder(s) the vivid and living elements of a world view. This is to say, it reflects the holder's investment in existence. In terms of it he defines to a great degree his life and his conceptualization of the nature of things.

The factor of emotional commitment is crucial. There is one and only one significant dimension of the religious,—that which stretches from commitment to indifference. A religious phenomenon is identified by the presence of characteristics of religious commitment, not by association with particular beliefs. Catholicism has consistently been well aware of this, as have wiser elements of less experienced ecclesiastical traditions.

To make clear the dilemma of American history it must be understood that metaphysics and religion are not separable in a living society, that they are not co-extensive but rather are contiguous stages in the major dimension of meaning, that their articulation is direct, that the dimension expresses itself in secular realms as fully and as readily as in realms associated with 'religious' traditions. Education, perhaps especially in America, has been a focus of contention precisely because it expresses so directly how people care about children and ideas. American cultural experience has been so to speak spitted on the point of just this problem. Education has meant beliefs about the real (metaphysics), and heavy commitment to one or another resolution of the problem of what to do about the real (a religious phenomenon). Because of national size and burgeoning cultural development education has also come to subsist to a degree in its own right; this too is a characteristic of religious functioning. The American dilemma with education is statable as a dilemma in the realm of religion because of America's national concern with separation of church and state. The dilemma is most sharply put as an issue of education and religion rather than merely as an issue of education and metaphysics, which of course it also is.

To review, then: since education is also a metaphysical expression a good deal of educational thought and practice is therefore religious in character, especially when marked by strong emotion as is commonly the case. Religion then becomes a powerful component in education. It has always been so, though infrequently recognized as such; there is no prospect that a secular society could be constructed in which this would not be so. In the nature of life it must be so. How then does the present age inherit so virulent an issue in the relation of religion and education?

It may have been an accident of history or an historic error in judgment. Certain of the American colonies took on predominant ecclesiastical positions; the Congregationalist Bay Colony sent its most distinguished Baptist into exile in Rhode Island "in the dead of winter." Other colonies had a range of religious pre-judgments. Toleration was rare, seemingly not a part of many plans for the new world. As religious conflict threatened to become sharper it was politic to evolve a separation of church and state, of religion and education, as a means of restricting the regions of disagreement. It was possible to resolve a good many societal problems and to achieve pragmatic solutions if their religious dimensions could be disregarded.

Notice that when a pragmatic separation of religion and education has been achieved American society undertakes to manage a fundamentally religious concern while wholly ignoring the religious character of the concern. This is a ridiculous policy. To attempt to resolve religious questions while ignoring the religious nature of the questions is absurd, to put it baldly. Even if it represents a worthwhile adventure in cultural understanding over the period of American civilization, which may be the case, it is still patently absurd in any final sense and it should not be expected to endure indefinitely without substantial modification. During the period of the American adventure solutions reached through separation of church and state have of necessity been achieved through religious compromise, acknowledged or not, and as solutions could only be temporary. When the religious nature of the original questions in education is finally granted the issues will come again before the people, their tap-roots better known.

Grant that American society has evolved an ingenious method of avoiding religious friction in education and has made of it a constitutional principle. The effect has been to enable a good deal of material and social progress in an immediate way at the expense of grappling with basic issues. From a pragmatic standpoint this has been useful. There is now better housing and more advanced transportation. Schools are learning how to teach mathematics and other studies in better ways, and there are more schools teaching these things in better ways. All of this has genuine value. It is better to have the housing and the transportation, the schools and the learning, than not to have them, other things being equal. At the moment "other things" are still more or less equal, mainly perhaps as a consequence of cultural lag. It is not clear how long they will stay equal, or when the conditions of life will demand that the fundamental questions of metaphysics and morality which are so profoundly involved in education and in politics be raised again. Conceivably the national upheaval over racial equality in the decade of the 1960's, a full century in the making, constitutes the summoning of a demand-note in the sphere of moral life. Not unlike our little moon in its staid and steady journeys around the earth the great American value-structure shows signs of wobble.

Why should this be so? A good part of the moral inheritance of the present time or for that matter of any time consists of what the time takes for granted from its own past. A time accepts and assumes this inheritance and functions in the light of it, but in taking it for granted it forgets to develop means for communicating its assumptive material to the third generation. Changes in belief and commitment consequently occur in the passage from the second to the third generations by the accident of omission. Some useful values undoubtedly inhere in this, in the enabling of new metaphysical and moral configurations. Some loss must also inhere in a type of change which occurs so much by chance. Accidental change in metaphysical outlook and value-structure brought about through geologic faults in communication, the fractioning of world-views in a three-generation period, must simply be re-examined from time to time by categorical re-orientation, in the light of fundamental reflective points of reference, whatever these may be.

American reflective thought must already have entered upon this great task. The major religious groups are at last beginning to speak with one another on basic issues of thought and learning, and this after generations of near-silence such that one tradition hardly knew what positions others took and rarely developed any acquaintance with literatures of thought other than its own.

And so it is that education stands forth as what it has always been, a fundamentally religious concern. It is religious because of the concern of education with philosophies of human nature, and through these, with philosophies of the real. Educational theories and practices are concerned with assertions of the real; they constitute the end-continua of metaphysical positions. If the beginning is made with educational theory the corresponding metaphysic is implied. If the beginning is made with a metaphysics the corresponding educational theory is implied. The envelope for all of this is the world-view, a complex of assertion and expression which is at once the common ground of religion and education.

Has American national policy then compounded an historic sport in excising religion from the public schools? It appears so. Education is of the nature of religion, but religion has been excluded from the nation's schools. What could be more ridiculous? Inevitably one is reminded of Washington Irving's headless horseman who rode forthrightly off with his head in the crook of his elbow.

Civilization is indeed gigantic guesswork, a function of which is to make trial of ways of thought and practice. Perhaps it is America's responsibility to try out the separation of education from religion, at least in a superficial sense. The effort may have still some time to run. In the long view there will be no great harm in continuing it. A national culture or two may decay or be destroyed; a few value-systems may tumble into ruin. Perhaps a civilization may become archaic, as so many have before. Life goes on; the contentment or misery of individuals or generations may not be the ultimate focus of existent natural and social energy. National decline and personal despair may have to be seen in perspective sufficiently long in purpose and time.

For the present America is coasting on its moral momentum. It is going as far as it knows how in the direction of cutting off its sources of moral commitment, which means that it has no alternative to moral drift. Inherited or residual morality remains of some use but there is necessarily some decline in ethical sensitivity because of the severing of the sources of originality in moral thought.

If it is true that American society chose an exit of convenience in its constitutional principles simply to avoid a great deal of conflict over religious beliefs, clearly no resolution of the issues can be foreseen which does not first provide formulas for practical handling of religious issues in the small community. Prior agreement at crucial points is a requirement among religious groups covering the objectives of religious study and religious association in school life, as well as on procedures to reach the objectives. A region of prior agreement should enable a community to function usefully in its schools even in the face of a high degree of local friction over religious issues. Ranges of choice should be open for local decision beyond the framework of common agreement to allow for new formulas and original solutions of inter-religious problems.

America here ventures upon new and untried ground. For a long time, as national histories go, it has been the public custom to look away from regions of religious belief, which is to say, from the fundamental issues of life and of nature. It is as if the greatest of countries had feared its capacity to face openly and in concert with itself the most profound and far-reaching questions of meaning and significance; it is as if it had dreaded to discover that its national integrity depended upon its collective ability to ignore what meant the most to its individual citizens.

In fairness to the past it may help to remember that the problems of religion with which America is now confronted are those of the colonial period augmented by the influences of later times. In the encounter of society with religious questions America at long last bends to the study of its own foundations. These were the challenges which our ancestors came here to resolve. Perhaps in the peculiar wisdom of history it was best that the nation should stand aside from this responsibility while awaiting the days of its maturity. Solutions to problems of diversity in belief can rarely be achieved through the use of force, although force has had its roles in the long history of belief. All too often where the souls of men have been at issue it has been difficult to know how to respond to religious opposition other than in some abrupt and helpless way. Colonial times were open to this error; three hundred years may not be too high a price to pay for increase of wisdom. In choosing its long detour America supposed she was evolving a lasting answer to religious diversity. This may not have been so. As education is of the nature of religion the choice which America made was a religious choice even in the midst of its seeming secularism, a choice marked by ephemerality, useful for a few centuries at best. No choice was possible which was not a religious choice. Colonial America then chose to avoid the risks of immediate struggle, to love with a pragmatic solution, with a religious disability which might well have no future of its own. In some unknowing way it may have done so the better to marshal its vast resources toward resolution of the profound and awful questions of existence.

America may have chosen well in those early times. Who among us could have chosen better? But the nature of man is irresistible. In the course of time he reflects, chooses to live more closely with his own nature and with the ranging universe. It is the choice of danger, but he chooses as he must. The questions of meaning are the great questions; they stretch to wherever and forever. They are insistent, demanding, challenging. For American civilization and for other cultures which it may serve the times may be near when they will no longer brook denial or delay.

VIII   The Essential Identity of Near-Contemporary Cultural Movements

The world-views which men hold are composed very largely of assumptions which are seldom reviewed. Most intellectual traffic—indeed, the major burden of communication in general—is in terms of vernier differences among the characteristics of movements or periods. The reason for this is simple enough. If comparison is to be made among cultural movements or periods, for example, or for that matter among almost any units of classification, the sensible approach is certainly to disregard elements held in common and to define the units in terms of differences. Necessarily, this is what is done most of the time. It is part of the present sketch to suggest, however, that it need not always be done and that at times it is an error to do it.

Very likely the definition of ideas and topics in terms of differences may be only a stage of intellectual development, perhaps an early stage or an occasional stage which recurs when the work to be done is simply the classification of materials in accordance with an existing system. Conceivably, periods occupied with the filling out of existing systems of abstraction may be succeeded by periods in which the language or abstraction-system is altered.

Another way of saying this, as Fagginger Auer was fond of observing, is that in different periods of history the reflective questions being asked vary considerably. The twentieth century has interests quite different from those of the nineteenth and therefore attends to different problems. It does not follow that the questions of earlier times have been answered. Quite probably men's minds will return to them some day when it appears there is something to be gained by doing so. While sets of questions posed by a particular age cannot be precisely answered during that age and are not apt to be answered afterward, it must be remembered that reflective questions are not posed in order to be answered. It would be very dull if they were. They are posed in order to encourage wonder and so to give rise to other questions.

Why is this so? Probably the forms and methods of thought become influential when the internal necessity of the state of knowledge requires it. An intellective line may have run out, as for example when the impact of Darwinism has been felt not only in biological but also in social fields, giving rise to many kinds of philosophic adventure, popular as well as professional. Then in some subtle way the exploring minds of men turn to other modes of thought. Under such circumstances a review of the modes of thought may be next in order. To a degree this appears to be the case at present, as shown by existentialist questionings of the edifice of reason and by other instances.

A startling new element may now have entered the situation, however, the effects of which are as yet impossible to assess. An analogy for this may be found in the fact that the peaceful and cow-strewn hills of Vermont were, at certain remote spots, hollowed out for missile sites. In one way it is interesting to know that the Green Mountain State is indeed living in mid-twentieth century, as in fact it is, sharing in the singular developments of the day. In another sense an element of the bizarre is introduced in that the roar of rockets and jets contend with the distant tinkle of cowbells in glades of peace and quiet. To return from the analogy to the problem, the different element making itself felt in intellectual America is a renewed necessity for methodological review deriving from the social consequences of enormously accelerated communications. The condition obtains more and more all over the world.

In the recent past, as in any period made up mainly of the filling-out of patterns previously defined, men have, so to speak, looked out of their faces at the world they seemed to see, accepting as facts the characteristics which the external world presented, and, again in a manner of speaking, ignoring the enormous worldview within the self. The latter is the set of assumptions in terms of which one conceives that which is outside the self. Tillyard in England and Lovejoy in America have described comparable assumption sets for the early modern period in their respective classics, *The Elizabethan World-Picture* and *The Great Chain of Being.*

There has been time in the past to make assumptions and then at leisure to work through the conceptions of nature and society appropriate to those assumptions, following this with new or modified assumptions and still different conceptions implied by them, and so on, over and over. The question is now raised whether intercultural association may be reaching an intensity which outmodes the normal slow pace of intellectual evolution, the pace of change in the climate of heart and mind. It may be that understandings of ideas and of cultural commitments to world-views in terms of their differences simply cannot be permitted to remain determinative in the social wilderness of modern times. The survival risk may be too great. It may be imperative that intellectual process and reflective communication become efficient.

This is very likely an involved task although not a great one. The tools and materials are in hand. The twentieth century is able to apply its aptitudes for the solving of many kinds of problems to those of the fields of general and social understanding, if it wishes to do so. Disagreement will certainly be vehement over formulations and solutions of given parts of these problems. Yet who will deny that cultural differences should be resolved to the extent that they cause interference with peaceful concerns on this odd celestial ball?

The consequence of the first point is that the pressure of social amalgamation on a world-wide scale has brought heavily and suddenly upon us a period of re-examination of the assumptions and procedures of thought—its forms as distinct from its particular and momentary content. This is the second major point to be made, and it will recur in the second section of this piece.

The statement of the problem then suggests that analytic or differential classification of cultural phenomena should be supplemented by an obverse view toward cultural wholes. Analysis has been and will continue to be a necessary tool but it is not an exclusive means to understanding. The enormous waste of intercultural conflict, actual or potential, could at least be made ridiculous—if not eliminated—through realization that common elements and principles apply in all the major movements of an age. To look for regions of identity among cultures and world-views may be indispensable now, in part to encourage social understanding and in part for the holistic dimension of thought. Survival of intelligence may depend on the possibility of thinking about cultural movements in a new way.

The quest for regions of cultural identity has longitudinal as well as cross-sectional aspects. Both types of relation will help to show the nature of cultural identification. For the purposes of this sketch, longitudinal identity will refer to the persistence of factors in the same cultural tradition over a considerable period of time; cross-sectional identity will refer to factors appearing in contemporaneous situations of seemingly diverse kinds. Notice that either approach carries the peculiar consequence that it is almost impossible to define precise lines of demarcation between periods or cultures. To leap from one century into another in the same cultural line or to jump from one culture more or less horizontally into another is to be reasonably certain of finding different conditions. But to show these differences is a matter of contrasting a nexus here with a nexus there. Even then the differences are largely those of constructional definition just as almost all knowledge is of the nature of constructional definition.

To turn to the definition of the elements of discourse as represented in the title of this discussion, the first notion of essential identity is intended to convey factors of thought, attitude and function which have large roles in any cultural complex, and which may be fundamentally identical with corresponding factors in other cultures. Cultural essences take a variety of forms from one cultural situation to another, but these essences retain their natures and can be regarded as constants. Numerous writers, for example, have found elements common to Christianity and communism; others have remarked in American society some modern forms of seventeenth or eighteenth century themes. The signal fact in cultural tensions may be that they hold in common very large regions of identity, albeit their several forms may also be inside-out with respect to each other. The question is what conclusions can be drawn from the identification and recognition of large cultural elements held in common among a variety of countires or periods of time?

Cultural movements, the second element of discourse, as a term refers to religious, philosophic, social, political, artistic, economic, scientific, national and international interests and activities, which, with related concerns in various combinations, make up the life configurations of an enduring society. The study of culture as a professional field is still in an early phase. Anthropological studies of particular cultures are now being joined by philosophies and even theologies of culture in general. There can be no doubt that studies on a cultural scale must become increasingly a focus of scholarship. As information continues to proliferate conceptual patterns of comprehensive kinds will be necessary to permit understanding of huge arrays of data. Divided subfields such as economics, psychology, physics, literature, and the like, will do well enough for analytic work. They are, however, mainly linguistic concepts or constructs developed on a small scale, already too provincial to convey a sense of reality on the enormous scale on which it is now to be had for the asking. By comparison with the new cultural perspectives the older constrictions of subject matter dangle weakly on their stems like withered fruits of a past season. The question here will concern the effects on investigative activities of the acceptance of very much larger conceptual patterns than have hitherto been developed.

The problem of time, the third element of discourse, is as involved as any other aspect of this re-description of knowledge. Various currents of culture certainly evolve at different rates. Within any one current some parts of it may move variously with respect to other parts. For comparison of factors among or within cultures the present thesis is that strict contemporaneity is not necessary. Differences in chronology of a century or even of several centuries might only disguise valid interconnections of materials. The central question in this area hinges on correspondences of substrata rather than on precise relations in time. That is, the question is what conclusions appear sound in the light of correspondences recognized as valid even across considerable differences in time.

Degrees of abstraction are found to be valid, and indeed, indispensable, in the study of cultures. Its complexities will require withdrawals to unfamiliar levels of abstraction, an order of discourse tedious for some who find it too vague for accuracy of definition and precision of detail. Nevertheless, objections of this kind are probably not relevant any longer. Where expansions of knowledge require the relating of huge arrays of data it is to be done through larger conceptual patterns and fields of reference. Regions of study have now to be recast in more comprehensive terms in order to add perspective. The reflective fields of religion and philosophy have long since faced this requirement and have responded, although with occasional periods of relapse into moods of analysis and reductionism. Scientific fields may have begun to face it, wanting mainly articulation with supposedly nonscientific fields. The social encounters of large populations, however, seem to provide the burning focus of the time even while they may provide only a different door giving on the problem of reflective and scientific fields. This may be where civilization stands in the balance, waiting upon whether it is to live or die. The stakes are worth the discomfort of altering antiquated patterns of knowledge.

To consider first a linear relation within one cultural continuum, it would be of interest if seventeenth century Puritan themes could be discerned in the supposedly secular society of twentieth century America. Assuredly they can. Forms of Puritan faith have been modified, but Puritan characteristics still shape American culture. Puritanism described the ruling power of earth as the absolute sovereignty of God. Every event was an act of God; on His will depended the smallest as well as the largest affairs. The reflective Puritan felt it his duty to ascertain the will of God and to live in accordance with it. In everyday terms this meant that the Puritan must work conscientiously at the obligations of this world. Although the Lord's will was inscrutable, if man's efforts fell approximately near to it the divine comment would appear in success at material affairs. The religious man was a prosperous man. How else would the will of God be conveyed to men? Private mysticism, a special way to the ultimate, was held to be dangerous, threatening the church and the established order of man's relationship to God. There had to be a degree of common agreement in the realm of religious knowledge.

The social group then was of prime practical importance in Puritan society, providing the ground of agreement on certain objectives and procedures. That is, although intellectual formulation of the Puritan position called for direct communication between man and God without mediation of human institutions, in practice the Puritan community did assert its right to approve or disapprove individual claims to religious knowledge. Religious certainty of community members had to be acceptable to other community members. Rational approval by the community was a part of religious normalcy. Antinomian difficulties arose over precisely this problem. Mistress Hutchinson claimed the right of religious certainty with insufficient deference to accepted grounds of certainty. What is the difference between her convictions and those of the flinty community which expels her? There is self-assurance on both sides and intractability on both sides. But the community agrees with itself and it has the advantage of numbers. Its grounds for certainty may be quite as irrational in an ultimate sense as are those of any individualistic mysticism, and indeed as nonrational as the ultimate ground of any reflective position when its foundations are traced far enough. The Puritan basis for acceptance of witness as genuine, in earlier days as well as after the retreat to the Half-Way Covenant, had to be agreement of the group on the nature of evidence. The community could tell when one of its number was going too far. Those who insisted on going too far were invited to get out.

A problem in evidence which arose late in the seventeenth century in connection with the Salem witch trials indicates the slow-moving but powerful influence of the social group. The convictions of accused witches in and around Salem were based on private knowledge, evidence which could not be confirmed from a modern standpoint. Evidence of alleged witchcraft had not been tested against the settled opinions of society for a considerable period. It was, in effect, a new situation without helpful precedents. In a remarkably brief time, considering the nature of the problem, the conscience of the community expressed itself through the judgments of prominent figures concerning the inadequacy of evidence relied upon in the trials, and the farce was ended. The same appalling error was never repeated in quite this form. Cruelty toward the innocent is always a desperately sad phenomenon, yet in few instances have the sufferings of only twenty persons effected so signal an improvement of the conditions of life for those who survived or came after.

Puritan beliefs in the absolute sovereignty of God, the direct relation of man and God even over the great gulf between, the elaborate rationalism on a remote basis of the nonrational, denial of the ability of the individual to achieve salvation without grace, and the influential role of community judgment—all can be found in subsequent periods of American culture. It is perhaps their configuration and particular forms which mark the earlier time as "Puritan" and some later time as "modern." To identify characteristics of contemporary life is a rash undertaking and not unlike quoting the Bible on all possible sides of some question at issue. Nevertheless it may be generally agreed that American society in mid-twentieth century is marked by stubborn individualism on one hand and on the other by a pervasive insistence on the validity of judgments made by the group. These contemporary traits may be obvious enough not to require argument. The forms of major themes can be expected to vary from one period to another. The idea of the sovereignty of God appears to be a factor in the reflective systems of contemporary America, either in the classic form of the idea or, if a sufficient degree of abstraction is allowed, in a variety of forms represented in systems based on a first cause of some kind—biological, physico-chemical, economic, philosophic, or of other sort. The sovereignty of God may have been replaced in some systems by a sovereignty of Something. Notice that the central idea of this sketch depends on the validity of interchanging varieties of first causes or ultimate grounds of action. The function of the sovereign God is fulfilled in a system which operates on the basis of another religious or of a secular first cause. Such variant systems may or may not be utterly wrongheaded, depending on the point of view. The present point is simply that they are comparable and may provide grounds for the recognition of continua which apply widely among cultural situations.

Precisely this interweaving of recurrent themes in a diversity of combinations and recombinations constitutes the ground for conceiving essential identities as characteristic of linear and cross sectional cultural relations. It is an interpretive issue whether a theme which is dominant in one form and one period and recessive in that form in another period, or the reverse, is or is not to be considered an essential identity. Similarly it is a question of interpretation whether a prominent theme disappearing in one form and reappearing, functionally, in another is or is not to be considered an essential identity. Until recently not much depended on interpretations of this kind. If it is true now that a great deal depends on interpretations of the nature of cultural movements, the meanings of cultural interrelations which have always obtained but which have not been useful enough to require much attention must now emerge from eclipse. Customary methods of defining cultural entities in terms of their unlikenesses may have to be turned inside out. The linear dimension of the thesis is presented in order to show the nature of the possibilities. It is interesting to reflect that the balance of individualistic self-determinism with social control by the group which is characteristic of modern American society is essentially a continuation of Puritan themes. For some it may remain an issue whether these recent ideas can be considered involuted manifestations of themes which were once

Puritan and before that were undoubtedly characteristic of yet an earlier cultural complex.

It is not the point, however, that cultural interrelations are mainly linear or that the historical dimension is the most significant one for understanding or for application in the midst of peril. On the contrary, the horizontal relation among near-contemporary situations, cutting radically across from one culture to another, may be far more useful in practical terms and may show quite as significantly the nature of the same problem of cultural relations.

To choose an obvious case from among many available on the front pages of newspapers, few large-scale tensions short of actual warfare have consumed as much energy as the Soviet-American stand-off in mid-twentieth century. Here are two cultures, or what pass for two cultures, with common origins many centuries ago; each having had ample opportunity for separate development, but considering America as part of the west European community, surely also having had a great many cultural exchanges, and still behaving with respect to each other as if neither had anything better to do than to fight. The Second World War appeared to end in the late summer of 1945; it was as if clouds had parted and the sun shone through for a few short months. Then the Fulton address destroyed the spell of peace, hammering on the notion that no real change away from war psychology was possible. Thunderheads rolled in again; the mid-century alignment of temporal powers assumed the familiar stance of endless opposition and stalemate. Countries and continents were affected; newly independent regions emerged into a power configuration in which the sides were already drawn. In this confused and depressing picture political and nationalistic oppositions are clear enough, but cultural conflict appears quite unnecessary. The opposition may be serious with serious consequences in the making, but there are not the earmarks of mutual exclusiveness which suggest that misunderstanding is inevitable. Soviet and other western cultures hold too much in common, historically and cross-sectionally, for there to be among them anything like intrinsic divergence. The notion of unavoidable conflict is probably illusory in this situation even though enormous proportions of energy are being consumed by its diverging vectors. The whole affair has the appearance of a contention within the house, a family squabble over details, which has no justification for existence in other than superficial forms.

Comparisons of Soviet with other western idealogies have often been made. Perhaps America is long since rid of the idea that there is anything substantially different, unique, eastern, or even Russian about the visible forms of socialist society. Centralization was not new to Soviet culture in 1917. It was generic to Czarist society. Crane Brinton has described the movement of power in a revolution from one social group to another and its eventual movement in reverse, perserving for the new social order the historic configurations of the old. But centralization has not been peculiar to Russian society. It has appeared in most countries of Europe and America at various times and may be a characteristic of certain cultural stages. In the United States it has come later, more gradually, and more gently, having developed less as a part of abrupt social disaster. Perhaps centralization in particular levels of cultural complexity may be followed by decentralizations on some regional basis which would unite advantages of efficient operation with those of originality and creative expression. This, however, remains to be seen, in America as well as in the Soviet Union.

To move from centralization of government to another instance: in America the locus of property ownership has changed for some public utilities and other facilities operated for public benefit which do not conveniently lend themselves to private responsibility under modern conditions. Transportation systems of large cities come to mind in this connection, as does also the federal insurance system for members of the armed forces. Various levels of state authority have been brought to bear in various instances. The Port of New York Authority is probably a form of public ownership. Government has taken an interest from time to time in the operation of privately owned utilities as well, as for example in the case of changes in telephone rates or where questions are raised toward the dropping of certain facilities for commuter travel in and out of large cities. Eastern Massachusetts was long entertained by arguments over branches of the Old Colony railroad, of which no spur or scheduled train was allowed to be abandoned before there had been consideration of the public interest, and so with other railroads in other places. These are motions toward social control within a private enterprise system. Motions in the reverse direction toward individual freedom and responsibility are also taking place within the socialist systems. In the region of civil liberties, where fundamental disagreement has been thought to obtain, Soviet society seems to be following in directions set long ago by Dutch, English, Scandinavian, and American cultures. Just as movements toward social control in America appear to be quite natural in the public interest and convenience, so do the movements toward individualism seem natural in Soviet society in what might be called the private interest. The Atlantic countries have reflected normal desires which men feel for increasing autonomy and self-management of personal life. Socialist society has perhaps reflected for historical reasons in the first instance normal desires which men feel for protection through the state against some of the hazards of disorganized existence.

Metaphysical differences between Soviet and Atlantic cultures may seem less readily reduced to essential identities, yet an interpretive reduction is possible. Russian culture was for centuries constructed around Eastern Orthodox Christianity, marked by ceremonial and other differences from Western Christianity but also by a general doctrinal coincidence. Following Brinton's thesis, when a culture overturns itself its major characteristics should be expected to reappear within the same culture and following the upheaval in forms which are perhaps new but still readily identifiable. In the vertical dimension this condition has been noted to obtain in the continued centralization of Soviet government, exploitation of large groups by small groups, the sacrifice of the individual to the state, and the like. There is also the cross-sectional relation which suggests that cultural characteristics cut across cultural lines, appearing in varied forms in cultures which think of themselves as quite different from each other. Doctrinal orientation toward a conception of a sovereign ultimate may serve the purpose. Soviet ideology denies the Puritan and Catholic thesis of the sovereignty of God. In place of the western conception of deity socialist society asserts the notion of the material first cause, the economic "means of production," which may be said to move things around. Functionally the two conceptions serve the same end. Each contains a representation of fundamental reality; each provides an explanation of underlying process; each enables its believers to relate effectively to its own version of the universe. Soviet culture may consider Atlantic culture to be the victim of a religious mirage; Atlantic culture may be convinced that Soviet culture is the prisoner of metaphysical self-deception. Yet each culture acknowledges an ultimate reality and relates effectively to it. Socialist reality is Christian reality turned inside-out—material substance or process established as final in place of spiritual substance or process. Socialist thought may tend to disregard certain questions concerned with the origin of things which traditional or Christian or even humanist thought feels justified in asking. But to disregard "final things" or to refer to them only by implication is not to abolish them, and to answer ultimate questions in a different way is to acknowledge ultimate reality in some form.

Atlantic and socialist cultures are doing most of the same industrial and technological things. Perhaps this very fact is a source of rivalry, but if so it should be the rivalry of courtesy and mutual respect and not a source of distrust. Outer space has room for all the rockets earth can produce; if some day there is traffic congestion around the moon and Mars there will be time enough to establish patterns of travel in space and to secure the cooperation of interplanetary vehicles. The immediate problem is very likely also a transient one—to avoid the consumption of human energy in overt conflict on the surface of the home planet. Soon enough the excitements of interstellar exploration will beckon to man's restlessness; perhaps the majesty of the heavens will end forever the need to engage in fruitless wars.

Notice that the characteristics brought to bear toward the thesis of this sketch may also be interpreted in the reverse way, supporting the contrary position. To illustrate with one of the suggested topics: the socialist description of ultimate reality as economic process may be conceived of as radically different from the Atlantic definitions of ultimate reality as spiritual or natural process, if the differences in form are defined as fundamental. If formal difference is fundamental difference, then the chasm may be absolute. If however there is a level on which two divergent systematic forms can be held to operate to the same purpose and in ways closely related to each other, the basis of intercultural relations may be of the order of essential identity, and therefore less limited in possibility. This is the present thesis.

It is doubtful whether any particular philosophic system is necessary to the validity of the idea of essential identity of cultural contents. A philosophic issue may be implied in the conception of cultural factors as constants, as suggested in the definition of the elements of discourse earlier in this piece. Constants, however, are familiar in most fields of thought and perhaps will not constitute a difficulty. Scientific and mathematical fields are replete with constants.

The usefulness of abstraction is beyond question, and it is precisely the phenomenon of abstraction which is indispensable to a synthetic approach. Conceivably the precise nature of abstraction may be subject to dispute and of great interest as a straight philosophic issue. But very likely the abstractive process is useful enough for most reflective procedures so that it is unnecessary to contend over it unless for the pure pleasure of doing so.

What is left is the decision as to which interpretation of intercultural relations is more nearly right. The facts of the matter are not likely to cause argument. Most students of culture will probably agree that eighty-five percent or more of the content of successive cultural stages in the linear or vertical dimension is common material. A like assertion in the horizontal dimension may be debatable, but perhaps not so very debatable either. The question turns on a point of meaning. According to one view, cultures showing different formal realizations of common concerns are irreconcilably different. Understandings among them will be possible but within the limitations imposed by a relation of opposites. According to the other view, cultures showing different formal realizations of common concerns give local expression to general principles and interests. Understandings among these may not be easy to bring about, but at least the ground for association becomes clear, and—when the stakes are high as the sky and round as the world is round—the basis for conflict is lost in a puff of absurdity.

IX World-View as Ground of Morality; A Phase of the Metaphysics of Education

By devious means one is led to the study of great questions. Philip Jacob's little volume, *Changing Values in College,* some years ago noted the lack of influence of American colleges on the values of college students, by implication summoning for re-inquiry the classic relation of metaphysics and morality, the nature of the real and the grounds of choice and conduct, which is to say, the springs of moral action. If choice exists, from what does it derive? Are personal or social factors involved in choice? Are the reasoning parts of life of small account, and is intellection itself a cerebral pastime not related to decision? Does morality perhaps depend upon the total view one holds? And does education have anything to do with values and commitment?

The Jacob study suggested on the basis of extensive surveys that American colleges have almost no influence on the development of ethical values among college students. Except for a few institutions with particular characteristics and effects of minor sorts, higher education appears not to be formative of moral positions among young people. Students tend to bring their values with them to college. They may conform somewhat to a self-centredness common in college communities, but otherwise they seem not to alter their values appreciably in any direction as a result of college life. The Jacob survey indicated that American college young people are contented with things as they are, tolerant of diversity among others, amiable toward government demands, religious in a detached and insignificant way, and moral, assuming elbowroom for moral deviation. The type of college curriculum, whether liberal arts, teacher education or other general education, seemed in the Jacob study to have no bearing on establishment of moral standards. Popularity of teachers also had no appreciable effect on value change or value acceptance; teachers might be liked or disliked; students did not accept their values. Teaching methods might have a slight positive effect if there is student participation in educational process, but this is not of much consequence. In short, according to the Jacob survey no identifiable pattern of general education appears to influence value change in the populations of American colleges.

Now all this is rather an ungainly camel for a college to swallow. Any educational institution likes to think that it graduates citizens and scholars of socially developed kinds. If American higher education is to be bailed out of this unhappy situation an assessment of the moral function of education will be needed to uncover the grounds of moral process and the ways in which education participates in it, if it does. It may be that our conceptual gears are slipping; perhaps it is simply a question of understanding the moral dimension or the moral consequence of learning.

Whatever the range of possible answers, the questions alone are enough to set the mind racing. Should classical theories of ethical motivation be reconsidered, as Socratic reliance upon knowledge of the good, or Christian dependence on grace or inspiration? Are American colleges incapable of providing more enlightened generations for the time "when our present ministers shall lie in the dust"? What is the moral work of colleges and how ought it to be done? Do churches and other institutions loom larger in the ethical prospectus because the moral efficacy of higher education has been doubted? Perhaps colleges and universities should rescind their claims to be formative in the fields of citizenship and moral education. Or perhaps understanding of the moral process will establish the role of the college in this sensitive realm of concern.

A departure point may be convenient, considering the intense interest which education engenders in American culture, and the sense of local responsibility which people have for it. The position to be taken here is that a deepened conception of the "world-view" stands as the fountain and the source of each man's system of moral vectors, that this complex conception of the nature of things is the indispensable matrix of value for individuals and cultures. To understand the value positions being taken in a given period the student must be able to move in and out of the world-views involved with each position. To be morally effective education should be free to work with the metaphysical implications of ethical viewpoints—which is at once to recognize that metaphysical positions are inescapable foundations of moral principles whether or not they are commonly attended to, and to suggest that the major reflective conceptions of the nature of things also have ethical consequences which must be taken into account.

Temperament and World-View

To William Ernest Hocking of Harvard University we are indebted for the currency in English usage of the German term which is often rendered "world-view," by which is meant a comprehensive conception of the universe with interpretive entailments. A pecularity of the human mind is that it wishes to know where it is, and it is in recognition of this trait that a re-emphasis on the idea of the world-view seems most in order.

An ant does not know that it lives in "Vermont," or that it is "lost" on a table top three feet above ground. Nor does it care; but curious reflectives of more complex make-up, pausing to watch the ant, consider that it may spend hours circling on its high plateau without finding a means of descent and therefore waste a good part of its life separated from useful tasks it might perform. It is all one can do not to spend one's summers in Schweitzerian ecstasy, picking lost ants off the tops of picnic tables and putting them back where they belong.

Man insists on knowing things in his own terms. He demands to know how the bluebird flies and where the wings of the albatross brush the southern seas. He devises geographic names and places and constructs ingenious grids of latitude and longitude no parts of which are of any concern to a bird which simply goes where it should to fulfill its cycles of existence. A bird may indeed be astromoner enough to fly at night by the stars, as the German ornithologists say, but only the restless spirits of men group the stars into pictures and spin legends of the morning of the world.

Man is dissatisfied without constructional knowledge of his own making, and he must build reference frames for the gathering crumbs of information which would otherwise lie scattered and devoid of meaning. It is assertive knowledge that he constructs but it can be reliable and repeatable— for the sensible reason that it is made so as to be both. And his knowing grows until its webs envelop most of the available phenomena of a time. He contemplates himself and studies his role in the universe. Without a comprehensive view his particular opinions have no meaning and serve only to get him from one day to the next as a fungus films over the surface of the land. World-views, the fine-spun theories of totality, are then the enablers of knowledge, patterns which make sense of the casual data of perception. In a manner of speaking everyone must have by implication a world-view, though not everyone need be concerned about it or even be aware of having it. Without at least a partial web of interrelationships the simplest day's existence would be fractured, filled with the 'crash-ups' of circumstance and conduct as when in a game of blindman's buff a child stumbles about a familiar room not knowing where to put hand or foot.

To be sure, the effort to form or re-form large conceptions of things has often been condemned as time-wasting mental gymnastics, lungings after vacancy, traps set for a moonbeam. But human nature is difficult to turn aside; it will do what it likes when it likes. And again and again at appropriate stages in the history of ideas the demand goes forth for the meanings to be had from the construction of immense cathedrals of the mind, the towers and arches of which give recognizable substance to the reaches of the universe.

Acknowledgment of the significance of the world-view requires a deepened conception of personality. Why should this be so? The subjectivist moods of the 20th century—linguistic, positivist, existential—may fall short of contributing to understanding through the architectonics of general ideas, but for all that they may singly represent distortions of the fullness of things still they may be phases of an emerging recognition of the significance of human nature conceived of as lens or focal approach to the real. This is the burden of Bridgman's statement, *The Way Things Are,* and it would seem an acceptable conclusion to draw from studies which bear on the impossibility of eliminating the individual from any part of the work he does, even from his most determined struggles toward objectivity. It may be fair to say that only by conceptual means, that is, through individual intellection making use of available evidence, can the real be known, and then only in part and subject to revision. If this is so, a variety of attempts to re-examine the composition and reliability of human experience may be quite in order, and such attempts do seem to be appearing in the several subjectivist schools. If it is true that the real can only be approached conceptually and individually, then clearly the make-up of human nature is of primary significance. For on that initial human reality will depend the type of evidence concerning objective reality which one is prepared to consider, and the world-views or conceptions of the total universe which are permitted to emerge as sovereigns of thought and action.

The notion of the world-view seems to demand as well a revision of priority among its elements. The natural world alone, conceived of in any of the usual dimensions of scientific investigation—physical, chemical, biological, social, or related orders of description—almost certainly does not exist. These abstractions are convenient as informational building blocks and materials for communication among persons engaged in certain kinds of useful work. Scientific descriptions of reality—as the term is commonly taken—are too limited in scope to be more than misleading oversimplifications. Many have known this for a long time, but habits of thought are strong and difficult to dislodge and it is quite another matter whether the general outlook of the mid-20th century with its persistent emphasis on "the world out there" is within reach of the realization. Yet the present intellectual movement is surely toward a new synthesis of the major fields based in the first instance on a common conceptual method of knowing, and recognizing the requirement of a comprehensive conception of human nature without the diffraction of which any general idea system will be unclear.

The individual person is to be conceived of as a unified spiritual, intellectual, emotional, and biological temperament, capable of immense achievements of extents and degrees unknown and thus far unapproached. The biological and emotional interpretations of human nature have inevitably been over-emphasized, the former as a function of the outstanding accomplishments in medicine and related fields, the latter as a consequence of the recent grasp of the importance of emotional problems and the development of psychiatric remedies. Intellectual and spiritual human nature, repeatedly denied its role in determining thought and action, has now to be restored to a controlling position in recognition of the assertive character of knowing.

The idea of man's spirit, a conception of human nature in its most comprehensive form, long ignored in the notable disfashion of the time, depends on awareness of the complexity of human nature itself as imperfectly approached by the narrower conceptual fields when they become broad enough to escape their self-imposed limitations. Appreciation of spirit involves a reversed-field understanding of the human situation. Man is not the extruded accident of natural process, picking among the offal for his sustenance, beating plaintively upon the doorways of the universe and crying to be taken in. He is rather the chief resident of the house, a simultaneous creator and discoverer, pattern-maker of histories and systems spun in the name of understanding. The alleged earthquakes of Wallace and Darwin and the impact of evolution in many fields of thought have never really altered the centricity of man. He was never dethroned. It is only that he has been very busy for a while with microscope and cloud chamber, asking new sets of questions and lining out new partial conceptions of the nature of things. Nor has the shift from the geocentric to the heliocentric to the astrocentric or acentric universe altered the significance of human values, since the properties and possibilities of the universe can be known only through the lens of human nature in all its simploid complexity.

It is not altogether comfortable to take a comprehensive position on the make-up of human nature, since in an age of remarkable discoveries it is the fashion to reserve judgment and to assume either that one cannot know what one is talking about or, if one insists on conceptualizing in spite of the risks, that one must use for the purpose no tools larger than a pair of stamp-tongs. The point in being adventurous is precisely that of taking as broad a position as can be formulated, both to encompass the available concepts of the time and, while providing for change and enlargement, still to enable the great potentiality of the general idea. For general ideas immeasurably extend horizons; they increase the awareness of possibility, and are fundamental to all kinds of significant development; without the general idea there can be only the grinding and bumping of the endless aeons, their flowers unseen, their birds unheard, their glorious sunsets dying forever over a thousand empty oceans.

World-View and Education

Royce S. Pitkin of Goddard College has suggested the likelihood of some intervening step in the educative process to explain the seeming ineffectiveness of American education with respect to values as reported in the Jacob study. He should not be blamed for hypotheses constructed from his insights, the conclusions of which might be far from his interests. However, some may speculate that such an intervening step may be the concern which education has with world-view conceived in its broadest sense as the ground and source of purposive action.

Connections can be said to obtain between major conceptions held by individual or cultural temperaments and the values which these temperaments also hold. That such connections do exist is a safe hypothesis derived in part from observation of the earnestness with which college age young people search for ways of life, and in part, like most operational assumptions, from constructional supposition. Subscription to values can be thought of as response to theoretical constructs recognized as principles or valid general ideas, or taken for granted without any recognition at all but existing nonetheless by concrete implication just as all facts or functions at once entail ideas and derive from them.

Education then becomes a dimension of individual development concerned with the construction of world-views and with response to them. In a more general sense education is everything that the self does with respect to what it considers to be real. Presumably no one in his right mind will be concerned any more with a definition of education as the precise transmission of material. The response of the student, his development, his awarenesses, his choices, and his taking of responsibility for his choices comprise the real challenge of education—from which it will be clear that the chief interest of the observer has to be the metaphysics of education—the conception of human nature as alive, assertive, replete with potential and with promise of responsibility, and the connections of individual temperament with the rest of nature, life, and spirit.

The Jacob survey seems not to deal with the metaphysics of education, or if its implications are to be acknowledged, to be seriously dislocated. According to its findings college-age young people have little positive concern for values other than those of conformity and avoidance of original self-commitment. The Jacob study can no doubt be criticized for its definitions and methods as was done by Barton and others, but the largest question surely follows from interpretation. A strange impression of human nature is given in the Jacob material. Young people are unconcerned with enduring values, it suggests; they are fun-loving indifferents; they are polite toward government, religion and morality as long as none of these confines their happy and conservative pleasure-seeking .... Are we to recognize in these implications the American young people we know? No college generation of our acquaintance has reflected such disinterest or unconcern. Rather the prevalent moods are those of earnest seeking, albeit the search is marked by sharp disagreement over goals, values, and methods of realization. Here must be the main ground of disagreement with the Jacob study. Either one trusts people or one does not. The Barton, Michigan, and other criticisms may argue over the social science methods of studies of this kind. But in a fundamental way the implications of the Jacob study appear to have gone abruptly out of focus. On interpretive grounds it has to be recognized as a distortion. American young people are simply not like that.

Without intending to judge with undue haste we nevertheless need not be concerned with the Jacob study beyond this point. For present purposes the useful topic is the relation between education and the construction of values, the concept of the world-view being interposed as the immediate concern of education from which in turn values derive as well as the capacity to implement value judgments.

What has been asserted thus far is the existence of a metaphysical bridge between valid general ideas on one hand and conduct on the other. The bridge always exists: idea and conduct always co-relate and each always entails the existence of the other. It cannot be otherwise, even when an individual may be confused about the actual world-view he holds or even unaware of it. The degree of confusion can be very high where the intellectual construct is not the same as the world-view, or where the world-view is not sufficiently general and does not include enough data to be valid as a principle. A world-view must be three-dimensional, obtaining in depth as well as in the length and breadth which are characteristic of a construct in the narrow sense. Evidently an individual may be imperfectly aware of one or more of the dimensions of his world-view; he may be restricted to a surface construct, or the depth dimension of his comprehensive position may be affected in bizarre ways, as described by Laurence Kubie in his *The Neurotic Distortion of the Creative Process,* so that the construction which results may be crystallized into monstrous shapes the parts of which are under great tension and subject to fracture. The physician of personality must replace the educator when the dislocation or tension become too great.

Notice that the present viewpoint is based upon a conviction toward the conceptual nature of knowledge. As observed elsewhere, this involves a certainty as to the concreteness of the general idea, its capacity to initiate action and to affect the world of things. This being so, the potential of education to contribute to the positive formation of life is substantially clearer than it can be in the nine-pin theory of human nature, in which individual lives are defined merely as vibrant plasmic receptors waiting to be bowled over by some wandering ion. To be sure, education worth the name requires a trust in people. To realize its immense potential education also requires a grasp of the nature and function of the general idea and of its place in the multi-dimensional awareness which is the world-view.

The danger in all this may as well be noted. A particular world-view or the view of a given period may become an end in itself, seeming to demand that its form be maintained without reference to ideas changing around it or to conditions being altered in response to new ideas. The danger of idolatry is as immediate for a comprehension as for another kind of image. World-views must be capable of change even though they are so laborious to develop that each successive mansion of philosophy appears to have been built for all eternity, immutable truth embodied in its soaring towers. But many a majestic edifice has been dismantled before the moss had time to gather on its northward side. The wrecker's ball is less respectful of the architecture of the mind than of more solid buildings. The philosopher who defends a system for its own sake will simply have his pate cracked for his pains. Education, being concerned with more than surface systems, with understandings in depth as well as breadth, must attend to the world-view, and to its dependence on a functional conception of human nature as a means toward metaphysics and toward metaphysical change.

In the latter connection repetition of a brief excursus may be of interest. Some years ago Bateson and Mead reported the attribute of "resonance" in describing personality. Speaking of the war-time problem of morale, the degree of commitment of persons to a necessary task, they suggested the idea of "latent morale" as being nearest the mark. Transfer of attitude, they felt, is best thought of not in terms of infection or contagion but rather in terms of resonance. In this view human nature is considered as a resource, a reservoir, in which the necessary elements and potentialities are already present. It remains in a given case simply to energize selected tendencies in people according to the demands of situation and time. There is no problem here of passing truth from an old skull to a young skull. Information may be conveyed from time to time but is not fundamental and can be handled in offhand ways without getting into the essence of education. Human nature is better seen as capable of responsible self-development among selected conditions and possibilities of choice. Reflective questions are not answered in this view any more than in any other view: undesirable attitudes can (perhaps) be resonated as easily as constructive attitudes. The moral problem remains. The Bateson-Mead theory of resonance merely specifies the full complement of potentiality contained in each individual life and the process by which development of attitudes takes place. While it had to do with the problem of morale, particularly in war-time its implications for educational theory in general will bear study.

The Morals of Humpty Dumpty

The points have now been sufficiently made. It remains only to refer again to the predicament common to ethics and education when human nature is conceived of as an extrusion of natural process in a narrow sense. This is a ridiculous problem. Man invents machines to control the world and devises at the same time systems of thought which deny his capacity to invent such things. What kind of ethics can contribute responsibly to life which is defined as irresponsible? And what is education to do when it must begin by acknowledging its inability to do anything? There is an old saying from the hills that some days it is not worthwhile even to get out of bed.

To return to the positive dimension, the immediate concern is that of increasing the region and the sense of moral responsibility, and in this concern education is commonly expected by the public to have an immense stake. To be sure, education does involve the central streams of human existence, yet the rationale for the concern is not always clear. If the articulation between education and moral behavior is indeed by way of the world-view or total conception of reality, a good deal of the American public interest in education becomes understandable. The essential substratum in this region of thought is the metaphysics of education, conceiving of metaphysics as the definition and description of the real, whatever that may be, and therefore asserting a major concern of education to be that of enabling young people to meet questions of a reflective nature which underlie the so-called practical problems of our age. Here is the basis for reflective studies of many kinds, as distinct from cook-book courses full of how-to-do-it recipes.

A conception of individual autonomy within the larger setting is demanded to account for the human situation. The 20th century view of human nature as a by-product of natural process simply will not do. The scientific order of discourse remains a subjective, dependent language invented by men for the purpose of saying something desirable and useful. Before it could become a completed construct it was already outmoded by the idea of human nature as a responsible nucleus of conceptual and perceptual activity, able to make judgments and decisions, the moral dimension of which is a reasonable ordering of life in accordance with understood reality.

Curiously, the traditional and liberal religious views of man and of man's place in nature, conceived of in their essentials as effectively the same, are the views which allow to human life the necessary freedom of decision which it must have if existence is to center successfully rather than blindly around the inevitable local foci of significance. Even the closest philosophic relative of religion, the so-called scientific view, is more deterministic and less able to provide opportunity for responsible self-development. Determinisms of any kind remind one of that mythological reptile, the educated hoop-snake, rolling brightly by with tail in mouth and mischievous eyes alight, having no end and no beginning and no sensible interrelation of its parts, and in addition no practical purpose in its motion. This is not quite fair, because reflective determinisms are by-products of attempts to simplify evidence and these do have pragmatic values. But a side-value should not be permitted to usurp the place of a balanced system.

If world-view is to serve as the effective basis of ethics and the moral life a developed conception of temperament is prerequisite to it, for the views one holds are necessarily filtered through the prism of the self, even constructed in terms of its characteristics. There is little argument over the responsibility of education for some part of the moral life. There may be a good deal of discussion over the ways in which education is to discharge its ethical responsibilities, assuming that it does have some. An integrated rather than a fragmented conception of personality seems to be a prime requirement for the development of world-views which are the indispensable foundations of morality.

X Communism as Religion

Conflicts, as noted earlier, are oftener described in terms of the oppositions of their participants than of their similarities. An idea is loosely said to be opposed to another idea; a social institution is "diametrically opposed" to another. Whether such expressions mean much is dubious. The whole view of a conflict is perhaps a function of the similarities as well as of the oppositions of particular contestants, since likeness of method and objective helps to define the disagreement. As the oppositions are usually well considered, it may be useful to attend briefly to the similarities of two notable opponents.

Religions are often recognized by means of their objects of belief. A group believing in an accepted deity is apt to be credited with having a religion. The classification is one of general consensus. If, however, attention is directed toward religious behavior and forms rather than solely toward the object of belief useful insights may be obtained, though the method is but a temporary means of study. In such an approach traditional Christianity and communism—the two subjects of this comparison—appear as similar groups of devoted believers, acting and thinking in large measure alike, making similar assumptions, developing similar organizations—and acidly attacking each other.

One should not suppose that believers of either kind will appreciate the effort to compare them. Orthodox believers will not care to be disjointed from their objects of belief like drumsticks from a bird, and communists will reject association of themselves with "religion" in any form. Yet two facts remain: these groups are locked in combat—and they are very much alike. Do conflicts arise in history between institutions and groups more similar than diverse in composition and activity?

To most people in the western tradition a religion is a system of belief and action between man and God. From time to time religions have arisen which attempted to replace God with something else, producing one or another of the several varieties of humanism concerned primarily with man as a child of the ages. For these sects some new player on the cosmic stage must put on the mask of God and claim to pull the strings of natural process. Sometimes it is a vague conception of the Good toward which men are supposed to strive in conscious effort. Sometimes it is the mechanical and self-sufficient universe in which man is seen as an accidental passenger. There is always something, or there is no system. For communism it is the form of society which acts back upon man and molds him like clay. If only the human aggregation (so runs the tale) could be suddenly remade in the communistic form, human nature would be transfigured by its sculpturing influence. Economic environment is the God-fool of communism.

If communism and traditional religion are similar in that each possesses an effective deity, they are also alike in their respective views of man. For Catholicism to a large degree, and for Calvinistic Protestantism to a greater degree, man is helpless. Borne down by inherent sin, he can be saved only by God's gift of forgiveness, grace bestowed from above. Catholic man can help himself a little; Calvinistic man can help himself not at all; every event in life and nature is an act of God; salvation and damnation are alike foreordained.

Peculiarly, communism also passes a vote of no confidence in average human nature, denying the capacity of the great mass of men to lead themselves—the very proleteriat whom it would help and on whom it would build its state. Beyond a point, Lenin felt, the workers have not the knowledge or ability to help themselves. They must be shown the way by a few leaders gifted with special insights and abilities who step down from the middle class to manage them, as he himself did. Such revolutionary leaders, of whom Lenin was chief, exhibit the main characteristics of religious prophets, notably the conviction of absolute rectitude as against both enemies and more moderate rivals. The consequences of this will appear below in various connections.

Human nature by and large has an implication of evil for both Christianity and communism. For Marx and Engels, as for the church fathers, man in his present state has little to recommend him. That man can be saved by grace alone is the Christian theme. For communism only by the prior transformation of society would man's nature become respectable.

An inconsistency appears in communist theory which also obtains in both the traditional branches of Christianity. The average man is by definition helpless, and yet in practice he is found to work devotedly for the realization of his ideals. If the kingdom of God and the proletarian state are respectively due to come inevitably, and if the average man is defined as helpless, why do men trouble themselves? Well, they just do. This inconsistency runs through all Christianity except the liberal wing (where the conception of human dignity obviates it) and it appears in communism. Neither the traditional Christian nor the communist has a formal reason in his own view to work for his conception of a better world. Both do work very hard.

The parallel is further pressed in the common tendency of communism and the authoritarian type of church to insist on government by the enlightened few. This is an institutional consequence of the prophetic mood and should be recognized as a religious trait wherever it occurs. The relationship between prophecy and fascism, and the implications of it for the role of democracy, have perhaps been insufficiently examined in recent years with respect to both use and abuse.

In the matter of the elect, or persons chosen to be saved, traditional religion is wary of asserting that its leaders belong with those who are given salvation by virtue of their faith or conformity, but the implication is that this is so. The whole problem of individual access to truth versus institutional mediation of the truth to men is full to thorns. Again, the liberal wing of Protestant Christianity asserts the continuance of revelation or its equivalent in nature, history, and human life. For strictly traditional Christianity revelation exists finished and complete in the Bible, the Word of God—the work of religion being to understand and apply its meanings as these unfold and are discovered.

The counterpart of the traditional position is clear in communism. The air of finality which marks communist doctrines of dialectical materialism and social process, and the absolute insistence of communism on its own rectitude and on its institutional authority over the possibly divergent ideas of individuals suggest that contemporary communism is a fundamentally conservative type of thought best compared to the really orthodox wings of Christianity. Christian truth is in general contained in the Bible; salvation is through faith in God and belief in Jesus as the Son of God. Communist truth is in general contained in the writings of Marx and Lenin; acceptance into the community of the elect is through belief in the dialectical process and in the desirability and practicality of the communist state. The touchstones of belief are severally followed by appropriate required practices.

In communism, as in Christianity and Judaism, a large body of interpretive material or commentary has grown up around the law, taking on much of its authority. So thorough and so ardent is this endless mastication of accepted principles that the loose comparison with mediaeval scholastic argumentation comes inevitably to mind. In addition, communist doctrine, though barely a century old, appears already to be static. Authority is firmly attached to it. Deviation from it is permitted rather less than deviation in traditional Christian thought is permitted beyond limits prescribed by ecclesiastical authority. The degree of adherence to doctrine among the convinced and "overconvinced" disciples of Marx often seems to go well beyond the disciplined acceptance of orders and to involve emotional commitment.

The operation of authority in communism and in traditional western religion is a recurrent theme even in a sketch of this brevity, since it lies so much at the heart of both, whether in the literal sense or as implied in their common claim of sole access to significant knowledge. Besides tradition and the law the secondary or interpretive avenues to certainty relevant to communism and religion include prophecy and revelation. Here, as in other regions, a comparison will hardly be welcomed by believers, yet the similarities are plain.

J. W. Allen remarks of the Puritans that they were characterized by an inability to see how anyone could honestly disagree with them, and hence attributed dishonesty to all their opponents. A more apt description of the recent communist attitude toward noncommunists would be difficult to imagine. Any opinion contrary to Marxist doctrine is regarded as deliberate deceit for purposes of material gain and maintenance of class control. Fanatic self-deception of this kind, like religious authoritarianism, is also a religious trait marking the prophetic mood in an early stage, its assertive self-assurance built upon presumption of direct access to ultimate truth and a tremendous feeling of moral obligation to preach that truth.

The reverse attitude of traditional Christianity toward its communist opponent may be recognized as basically the same uncompromising commodity, but in a more advanced and mellowed stage in which the accumulated keenness of centuries of institutional experience tends to modify in some degree the underlying absolutism.

Perhaps no term applied to any part of communism could be less welcome than revelation. Communism would have its faith regarded as precise induction from observation scientifically conducted, its doctrines seen as based on laws observed to be working in history. The exact extent to which communist doctrines do represent the realities of social change must be left for definition by the social sciences and by the disciplines of history and philosophy. The philosophy of history is a highly interpretive subject, as its theorists have shown from Amos of Tekoa to Arnold Toynbee. Marx's patterns have already had to suffer modifications in the face of fact; evangelical predictions also commonly must. As Pauline Christianity had constantly to explain through its early centuries why Jesus had not yet reappeared in glory, so communism now repetitiously foretells the imminent dissolution of the West and the accession of the New Jerusalem of Marx to power. Apologetics are neither new nor merely old.

In any comprehensive theory of the nature of things some empirical observation is present. But observe that neither communism nor unmodified Christianity is concerned with the immediate and present world. Both reject this world in favor of a world to come. The Christian advent is presumed to be spiritual; the communist advent is presumed to be material. But both are worlds other than this one; both will arrive after a period of preparation and by means of a catastrophic passing of the present into the future—revolution in the doctrine of communism—involving elements of final judgment, disposal of nonconformists, and rule by the elect, corresponding to elements in the Christian conception of judgment and salvation. The eschatological nature of the communist idea is apparent.

How does anyone predict a world to come which is different in kind from the present world? Whence does knowledge of an ideal world derive? Christianity and communism alike assert that their respective ideal states have never existed on this earth. Can a totally other be forecast in terms of an actual? The ideal state itself and the means of reaching it must in each case be defined through faith.

Both traditional Christianity and communism claim to possess the truth and to be absolute in knowledge of significant things. In Christianity this knowledge is obtained by revelation through the Scriptures. In communism the type of knowledge is similar; reliance upon scripture is similar; the psychological process of acquiring certainty is similar. For both these schools the ordinary human individual is rarely influential; it is not clear even to what degree the individual can assist or retard the drives of history and environment. The problem of the new is the same for both Christianity and communism. True knowledge of new things has in one sense to come from outside the system, for the system does not contain it. Knowledge received by a system from outside is in effect revealed to it.

Christianity has long since realized the eschatological nature of its conception of the kingdom of God and has been enabled thereby to develop realistic "interim" policies for dealing practically and effectively with the affairs of this world instead of insisting upon direct and exclusive preparation for the second coming. Communism in its youth still has painful lessons to learn in this respect. The same realization is implied in its political philosophy of the interim dictatorship, but its day-to-day activities in the west are still largely millennial in character rather than realistic—in that they prepare directly for the advent of an ideal state which is by definition impossible of realization in mind or society, given the limitations of human and natural equipment. The disillusionment in store for young and sincere believers in the coming of the communist kingdom is pathetically great. If some communist leaders are emancipated from the idealism of the eschatological view and are interested solely in the interim objective of attaining and holding power at any price, even the price of destroying the genius of their movement, their efforts must merely be countered as any minor fascist threat is countered. By and large the treatment suggesting itself is that accorded to the sect of Jehovah's Witnesses: freedom to valve their steam, freedom of action insofar as it does not interfere with the freedom of others—and use of democratic methods to reduce genuine grievances which feed fascist causes. This aspect of the problem will recur below.

It will be understood that the genius of an eschatological point of view lies in its juxtaposition of the possible and the impossible, the practical and the ideal. This has in fact been the central compulsion of Christianity and the mark of its achievement throughout its history. Other things being equal, similar achievement awaits the similar movement which balances water on both shoulders in like manner. But it will not do for such a movement to relax into simple otherworldliness, or yet to forget the ideal for concern only with the immediate. History passes a sentence of death upon failure in either respect.

A brief glance at the likeness of communism to a church is now in order. The notion of such a comparison is not new, nor does it require much imagination to see the communist party as a variety of church. In communism the average man must submit to party leaders, and in orthodox religion to religious leaders. Discipline is required of each membership. Distinctive gradations of achievement and status obtain in both groups.

The existence of ritual and ceremony in French Revolutionary Jacobinism of the 1790's has been described by Professor Brinton in *A Decade of Revolution.* What formal rites are operative in the revolutionary cults of the mid-twentieth century? That there must be some in so tightly organized a group as communism may be supposed, whether or not they are recognized as such. Careful comparisons of persuasions-to-communism with conversions-to-religion have probably not been made; the existence of similarities can reasonably be suspected.

Guerard observes of Napoleon III that he stood for order as the first step in the establishment of the ideal condition of socialism. Some say that Napoleon III was the first of the modern fascist-type rulers; or, if he appears too gentle beside our Hitlers, at least that he was an early stage in the line of political development which produced the more accomplished dictators of the twentieth century. Certainly the prerequisite of order and discipline is a mark of the contemporary communist party on its several levels. Likewise in the demand of the orthodox churches for discipline prior to consideration of individual variation is perceived the prime element of order. The preestablishment of order would seem to be a general demand of absolutism, and should perhaps be recognized as a religious trait, at least in the traditional sense.

Obvious in Marxist literature is the moral indictment of a society newly dominated by the machine. So is it obvious in various sections and periods of the church. The presence of "concern," in the Quaker phrase, is again a telltale symptom of an operating religious psychology, whether within or without the recognized churches. The parallel runs even farther. The social quest of communism suffers from a negative, backward-looking mood of longing for the relatively primitive days of no machines, or fewer machines, or less complex machines; it is likely to oppose technological change as such on the basis of its immediate impact on labor, instead of studying methods of harnessing technological change in the interest of labor and of all concerned. Remark in this the antique theme of so many of man's religions, primitive and contemporary: the theme of the golden age, when the world was young and happy, and sin was not.

Stranger groups in history have been usefully compared to churches. The famous "new model army" of Cromwell's England behaved like a church in one period of its existence, but as a congregational-type church in which conclusions were derived from extended popular discussions in the ranks rather than exclusively from reference to superior authority.

The role of violence takes signal place in these reflections, since in its attitude to the arbitrary use of force a movement breaks out its true allegiance and the portent it holds for the democratic way. General Eisenhower comments in *Crusade in Europe* that the use of force is an extension of political policy. One might add: of any policy in which particular wills week to implement themselves in action. Mediaeval Catholic use of the Inquisition and Calvinist violence against sectarians were not accidents in the history of churches. Both were extensions of religious and political policy into "the field of force." Both are directly comparable to the communist attitude toward violence.

American Protestant sects in colonial times seem to have been driven into mutual toleration in part by their numbers and by the impracticability of domination by any one of them. Toleration may have become necessary less on principle than as a matter of mere survival. Protestants commonly assume that their churches have learned to get along without assistance from the state. Perhaps they have, but it is well to bear in mind that the Protestant churches have been in their historic origin fully as absolutist and uncompromising as any religious position ever taken. Precisely what the Protestant potential for intolerance might be, given encouraging circumstances, is a question not lightly answered. Many contemporary Protestants may perhaps be relatively unacquainted with the official positions of their respective churches, or with the implications of those positions.

Catholicism is said to be a series of different churches in different countries—French Catholicism one thing, Spanish another, American another. Regional practices vary; but in general with Catholicism as with Protestantism the use of force is no longer politic in this country, albeit American channels of communication are familiar with various forms of moral pressure. The potential of political and intellectual repression is a question with any religious position, and the lines of future development in these respects are notably uncertain.

For a group which asserts a unique relation to absolute truth it is logical to use force to wring conformity from unbelievers. After all, unbelievers are wrong; and to be wrong is evil. To burn a mediaeval heretic for the glory of God was also to do for the sinner the sober service of terminating his sin. Suppression of unsuitable literature is likewise logical, given the premise of special access to truth, to prevent contamination of the innocent reader. Is it far from this to the political and intellectual manipulation of the individual in behalf of the purposes prescribed by communism?

The degree to which communist absolutism parallels the religious is also seen in its attitudes toward more moderate groups of the left wing. The conviction of absolute rectitude on the part of an absolutist group is endangered by the activity of a moderate group which claims to traffic in the same commodity. Herein is rooted the studied anger of communists against left-wing socialist and labor groups which they cannot contrive in some manner to control. Such advocates of "gradual social evolution" undercut the absolute communist demand for power on its own terms by doing peacefully what communism declares can be done only by violence under communist leadership.

Certain conclusions follow from all this.

Like Protestantism and Catholicism, communism is one of the clearest absolutisms ever to stalk the boards of intellectual history. Ideas are, as everything else in the Marxist view, relative to and dependent upon economic conditions. But, as M. M. Bober observes, in *Karl Marx's Interpretation of History,* the relativity of ideas is not admitted by Marx to be a notion which is itself relative, subject to modification at the beck of changing conditions. Economic environment is the absolute in communist theory; and the construction of absolutes should be recognized as a traditionally religious type of thought, shielded from pervasive empiricism and the piecemeal assembly of evidence by the effort of the normative thinker to produce a consistent and particular result. Universalistic interpretations have their usefulness, and to them mankind will return again and again. But there is no excuse for not recognizing absolutisms for what they are.

Since Catholicism is foremost among the militant orthodoxies of the present age, continuing conflict is to be expected between it and communism. This war will be between groups having forms, methods, and some objectives largely in common. Of the two, insofar as physical violence is a thing of the past and in terms of the possibility of freedom through independence, Catholicism is to the liberal observer incomparably in advance of communism. An absolute system inevitably threatens a state of relative freedom in which the greatest number may strive for their conception of the greatest good. The position of a church on the problem of absolutism should be a matter of public record in a democracy. In recent years American Catholicism has faced these issues, as for example, in John Courtney Murray, *We Hold These Truths,* and in similar works. As between communism and traditional Christianity, communism may be considered as still in a primitive, early stage of development in which it has not yet learned to add compromise to its absolutism and to live in peace with those who disagree, relying upon methods of democratic persuasion to promote its viewpoint. Notice also the very different degrees of readiness to compromise which are shown in Soviet and Mainland Chinese communisms. The Chinese is typically the earlier developmental version. In general, of course, communist use of violence is much nearer the surface. Catholicism has the tremendous advantage of sophistication; and for all the risks of subtle pressure let it not be supposed that this restraint is without its value when open force contends with freedom.

Catholicism cannot help but feel that communism is a menace. Any highly similar but significantly differing sect has always been felt to be a menace to the main stem of Christian tradition. But it is difficult to imagine that communism could ever win against Catholicism. Overt attacks on Catholic leaders, whatever the undetermined rights and wrongs, have merely allowed the Catholic church to declare public war on communism, and have perhaps been a fatal error in recent communist strategy. Catholicism has had fifteen hundred years of experience in dealing with lay religions, dissident sects, and autocratic governments; it will be at no eventual loss in dealing with communism. And it will never give up, though centuries pass. Communism as a religion has no ultimate chance.

The lasting contribution to human thought which Marxist theory can make may well be first in its rational emphasis on the economic motive as one among the movers of history. For this enormous service mankind will owe a debt to Marx as great as that to Freud. Beyond this a deeper function will be performed. The communist emphasis on social change through fascist means will heighten the challenge to the west to meet similar problems through democratic means. The west must learn that to meet the political challenge of communism it must surpass it in political achievement of social ends. Thus by a kind of electriclike induction the greatest service of this latest of the schismatic sects will be rendered to the mother stem.

For the rest, the rational elements of communism will make a contribution as ideas of any kind should be free to do. The nonrational elements, while explaining much of its form and behavior and lengthening its hold on life, labor at a sharp disadvantage against older and wiser opponents. The difference between the relative durability of Protestantism and the brief life-expectancy of communism, both being considered in relation to Catholicism, lies in this region. Communism comes too late and feebly on the ground. Insofar as this is a religious struggle—which it is in part and only in part—it is an unequal contest of psychologies, and Antaeus will win against Hercules.

Observers of contemporary events should realize, however, that the war between communism and Catholicism is not the main show in the religious affairs of our time or of any time. The direction above all others in which a religion must expend its greatest effort is that of unbelief—indifference, secularism with respect to religion in general, utter lack of interest— not the direction of idolatry, which is religious effort in a different quarter. Religious activity of any genuine kind, whether within or without a recognized church, argues the presence of "concern", and traditional Christianity knows what to do with that. Conscientious paganism, in the long view, has not been the most formidable obstacle in the march of the Catholic church. The greater threat to an experienced religion continues to be indifference to all belief rather than the activity of an inimical belief.

Catholicism has certainly not diverted its major forces from the war against secularism to the noisy front it maintains against communism. Clearly, it will not have to do so.

XI Apparent Religious Themes in Contemporary Mainland China

If a civilization is indeed to be regarded as an enormous essay in idea and action, in patterns of order and in ways of doing things, a review of apparent religious themes in the thought of contemporary Mainland China offers certain possibilities. Referring to Mainland Chinese thought as that represented in Chinese Communism rather than in the thought of western, mid-Eastern or Far Eastern religious groups still existing in China, the purpose will be to examine reflections of a recognizable kind in such contemporary material as filters out to the West, to see whether or not they continue what have seemed to be very old Confucian themes. If it is true that so enormous a social group as the Chinese people, and so involved and so rooted a culture as the Chinese, could not be deflected from its course by very sudden or very substantial forces of change in any but minor ways, the observer of such matters would expect to find continuing themes even in what has come to be called the new China. This is the present hypothesis.

Several difficulties of course present themselves. As every reader of the Bible knows, in the study of a subject sufficiently complex it is possible to document almost any position by selecting the evidence appropriately. No doubt one could take either side of the issue of enduring themes in contemporary China and make a good case for it. There is also the problem of working with translations from the original language, when the reader may not be aware of implications which might obtain in original texts. A third region of possible disturbance we may rule out of account by defining things clearly: some say that Confucianism was or was not a religion, and some dispute the same issue with respect to Communism. In this sphere of concern the reference will be most often to a psychology or a system of attitudes characteristic of religion in certain of its phases. Insofar as use is made of this dimension any school of thought and action can be referred to as a religion providing the context is clear.

It is not politic, moreover, to be deterred from presenting a highly interpretive position by the considerable likelihood that the interpretation may be completely wrong. After all, what are arguments for except to establish the truth? The risk will be taken, whatever the danger. The literature also shows that the question is an old one, both sides of which have been often advanced and defended. The positions taken here are in the nature of modernizing a familiar problem.

If Confucianism is to be reduced as Joseph Needham reduces it to a single phrase, it may as well be his phrase. Confucianism was, he said, a doctrine of "this-worldly social-mindedness." Confucius lived in a period of "bureaucratic feudalism," (552/3-479 B.C.) undoubtedly accepting feudal social organization since there was no possibility of other forms of social organization nor of other sources of order. He saw himself as a transmitter of ideas rather than as an original thinker. Few formal schools could have existed in or before his time. What traditions he drew on it is hard to say, but there must have been some and they may well have been of long standing.

The major element which Confucius appears to have established, whether or not he originated it, was the dimension of personal morality and its application chiefly within the social realm. This double emphasis of Confucianism in all of its periods is reiterated constantly as its chief thematic complex. Its metaphysics has been a social metaphysics, if there is such a thing; its ethics have been personal and social; its divinities have been largely abstract, or at times have consisted of the Sage himelf and his followers involuntarily elevated into objects of veneration.

Through a peculiar division of Chinese society the leading elements of the culture were attracted to Confucian thought while the lesser elements, perhaps those more closely in contact with nature, became Taoist and developed the equally Chinese but less socially prominent involvement with the Way or the Order of Nature, and with the relation of man to this natural order. It was more from the latter, says Needham, that the very recent Chinese interest in systematic study of nature has derived, but there had to be long centuries of wandering among limited interpretations of nature, among magic and false philosophies, before science as we think of it could appear in China. Needham's point on

Taoism is that its attitude to nature has too often been put down to being only magic, whereas the genuine kernels of its attitude may have been missed.

These two traditions in Chinese thought have seemed to continue, the former a socially respectable philosophy separated from concern with nature and attending instead exclusively to human affairs, drawing its wisdom from human relations, assuming that reality is of the order of individual and social man—the latter less socially accepted but interested in nature, moving into magical and ritual interpretations of the relations of man and nature so that its potentiality for systematic study of nature was bound up for centuries by a combination of social and ceremonial factors. Karl Eskelund says that one of the things which the contemporary Communists in China have done is to restore the old Eastern medicine to an earlier status of social respect and professional standing. Perhaps if this is so it is an instance in which the Chinese Communists have re-expressed an ancient Chinese tradition, as they have in their universal emphasis on participation in manual labor, albeit in these two cases a Taoist rather than a Confucian tradition. Needham observes that early Chinese medicine was necessarily Taoist in origin, involving as it did manual operations which restricted its social acceptance.

The major Confucian theme seems to have been a moral one. The *Analects* are a collection of moral precepts and moralistic insights using as material the comings and goings of people and judgments about the conduct of people, actual or ideal. Accounts of Confucianism in recent literature often turn out to be accounts of neo-Confucianism, the period of 12th to 15th century rationalistic and idealistic re-thinking of Confucianism. There are probably practical reasons for this. Confucian literature which has come down to us from earliest Confucian times shows characteristics of original religious literature. It is gnomic, heavily worked over, extensively edited, in some part of uncertain authorship. Its setting amid feudal life of the Warring States is likewise problematic and subject to supposition. Under such circumstances knowledge of the cultural setting of scriptural literature is needed, and Confucianism as an interaction of reflective principles with a cultural setting reasonably well known is readier to hand in the great revival period of Neo-Confucianism which corresponds to our western awakening of late-medieval and early Renaissance times.

Summaries of Confucian characteristics may therefore tend to draw on an ancient and neo-Confucian amalgam. Confucianism as it came down to the twentieth century certainly was such an amalgam. Wing-tsit Chan describes its essence as the principle of propriety, with additional themes of filial piety, obedience, subordination of women, and a variety of mores, rites and ceremonies, such as elaborate funeral practices. Professor Chan writes with one eye clearly on the relation of Communist ideas to the religious themes of traditional Chinese thought. So does Amaury de Riencourt, and so no doubt do others such as H. G. Creel and J. R. Levenson. So interesting a possibility would not be lost on interpreters of contemporary China, although some have the historian's professional reservation against seeing patterns in history.

To compound the dubiety by applying to the 2,000 years of Chinese history the pattern of a religious philosophy of history, the lay observer concludes that the fundamentally moral nature of Confucian thought has in the course of time undergone a reasonably normal shipwreck as a consequence of excessive institutionalization. This is always the problem with inspiration, with moral force in its other-than-early stages. The moral commitment does not last; it must take refuge in institutional forms. The result is moral convention, perhaps even bureaucracy, with the decay which goes with formalization. But what is the alternative? No one has ever discovered how to inherit moral force or how to cause it to be inherited. The most that has ever proved to be practical after an initial moral force has spent itself has been a judicious alternation of periods of institutional support for morality with periods of moral reform involving renewed moral commitment on the part of at least some sensitive individuals.

The really remarkable question is how a morally oriented society could have endured as long as Chinese society did, with so few well-defined periods of major reform. The answer must lie in the peculiar composition of the routine or daily relation of the individual self to the principle of morality as expressed in Chinese social forms. There must have been enough of the sense of moral renewal in the normal course of moral exchange between what was and what should have been to level off the predictable alternation of inspiration and decay. The political and military conflicts of the States, dynasties, and sub-groups may also have absorbed some of the moral energy which Confucianism brought to focus.

Given a social philosophy closely tied to respectability, heavily moralistic, highly ceremonial, this-worldly, little interested in cosmology, and giving great emphasis to social expression of values in governmental and public function, what reflections of attitudes underlying these characteristics does one find in contemporary Chinese mainland literature?

Recent Clues from Mainland China

A word about sources will be in order. As American travellers regrettably have not often been allowed in China in recent years reliance has to fall to a limited extent on travel books published in Europe, and increasingly on social science research material coming out through Hong Kong, compendia of which are now being made available. Also useful for Americans is the *China Mainland Press and Magazine Surveys* and related materials, translated, summarized and published by the American Consulate General in Hong Kong and by other U. S. Government offices. For this sketch the *Mainland Press and Magazine Surveys* have provided most of the indicative illustrations.

Beginning with the theme of respect for tradition and the past, various expressions appear in attitudes to past events or in ceremonies given over to memorializing events or persons. Illustrations included here are summarized in paraphrase or quotation; the intervention of translation must be borne in mind.

"Shanghai Lu Hsun Memorial Building Opens"

.... Shanghai's first memorial building was set up at Lu Hsun's former home in 1951. Present Hung Kew Park Museum built in 1956, in the building style of the writer's home town of Shaohsing. Over 2,000,000 visitors including those from 71 foreign countries have visited it. There is a new bronze statue, and the words "Tomb of Lu Hsun," handwritten by Chairman Mao Tse-Tung, have been re-gilded. Reliefs based on Lu Hsun's own designs for the book cover of his work *The Grave,* are carved on the granite base. Trees and flowers that he liked have been planted around the tomb.
—SCMP, No. 2590, October 3, 1961

This suggests that the focus of memorializing may have shifted somewhat in contemporary China, but that the process of constructing a modern tradition is very active.

Other cases indicate similar interests:

"A Commemoration Meeting"
A commemoration meeting was held in Peking March 12th, 1953 on the 28th anniversary of the death of Sun Yat-sen, by the Revolutionary Committee of the Kuomintang. Local Shanghai leaders visited his former home there; Soong Ching-ling, his widow, visited "and presented flowers." Local officials placed wreaths at the mausoleum in Nanking.
—SCMP, No. 531, March 14-16, 1953

Memorial services are not infrequent in the *Press* reports. Several in 1953 concern memorials on the anniversary of an airplane crash. On April 8th, 1953 a service was held on the seventh anniversary of the loss of the "April 8th martyrs," killed in 1946 in a plane accident in Yenan (SCMP, No. 548, April 10, 1953). A nearby note (SCMP, No. 541, March 28-30, 1953) says that monuments have been carved in a rocky hillside at Sangkumryung for six dead members of the Chinese People's Volunteers. In March 1953 several issues are devoted to accounts of memorial meetings, studies of doctrinal literature, and pledges from many groups to make renewed efforts toward realization of common objectives, all following on the death of Joseph Stalin in Moscow.

A deliberate effort to cultivate awareness of Communist tradition appears in *SCM Magazines* in summaries such as this:

"Be A Most Ambitious Revolutionary"
by Yü Sui-an

(This account remarks how a new mass movement has been set off for the teaching of revolutionary traditions, by young people under Party leadership. The aim is to raise the "political consciousness" of youth and to promote revolutionary ambition for realizing lofty revolutionary ideals.) —"When we hear the old comrades who took part in the 25,000-li Long March telling their stories about the Long March, or when we see the motion picture 'In the Name of Revolution,' how can we not be greatly touched and excited? The large-scale construction of our mother country which we are undertaking today precisely has been made possible by the sacrifice of many comrades-in-arms and martyrs of the past...."

(The account goes on to tell about the revolutionary scope of ambition and problems left still to be solved.)
—SCMM, No. 257, April 17, 1961

Funerals of prominent political or military persons are mentioned with some frequency.

"Funeral of Senior-General Ch'en Keng, Deputy Defense Minister"

Senior-General Ch'en Keng died March 16th, 1961 of a heart attack. The body lay in state the first day, with flowers and greens. The family was present and guests came to pay respects. The body was sent to the crematorium at the end of the first day. A Funeral Committee of 34 persons was formed at once. On March 25th, 1961, nine days after death, a funeral service was held with 2,500 persons present. White scrolls were hung inside and outside of the auditorium. The cinerary urn and picture of the deceased were in evidence. Marshal Lin Piao presided; Senior-General Lo-Jui-ching delivered the funeral oration.

—SCMP, Nos. 2467, 2471, ca. March 30, 1961

Death of a less prominent person may be recorded as follows:

Obituary Notice of Sun Chien-Ch'u

... who died at Peking at the age of 55. A Funeral Committee of 27 persons was appointed. A memorial service and coffin burial were arranged, the service to be at Chia Hsing Temple, Peking. Elegiac scrolls and wreaths to be sent to the Funeral Committee at the mortuary within nine days after the service.

—SCMP, No. 458, November 22-24, 1952

Evidently there is a policy on the part of the current Chinese government to encourage cremation in urban areas. This is discussed in a notation from the year 1952, with the acknowledgment that different national groups have their own burial customs and that the government cannot determine in favor of one way of disposal of the dead as distinct from another.

—SCMP, No. 448, November 7, 1952

Ceremonial committees are apparently common for general or public celebrations. An item in *SCMP,* No. 2588, ca. September 27, 1961, giving the "Namelist of a Preparatory Committee for Celebration of the 1911 Hsinhai Revolution," notes a sizable committee of one chairman, 13 vice-chairmen, 1 secretary-general, 8 deputy secretaries-general, and at least 81 other members.

The most interesting category of evidence concerns the relation of the individual to his cause (or Cause), to a final force in his real world, or to the social medium with which he must align himself to achieve an effective relation with one or more of these ultimates. Here one is engaged in a study of religious psychology, of attitudes, and of modes of self-expression.

First consider the problem of the scholar who suddenly finds his world sliding under his feet. It is not easy to discover what is happening here. The case of Fung Yu-lan comes first to notice. In two articles excerpted in the *Mainland Press* Fung publishes his convictions (1) that the history of China since 1949 is fundamentally different from previous Chinese history (SCMP, No. 435, October 18, 1952), so that only now does it begin to conform to Marxist-Leninist historical laws, thus taking a first step toward a new philosophic position; and (2) that his own philosophic work in earlier years had been a major mistake and should now be corrected:

> "Change of My Ideology Since the 3-Anti Campaign"
> In this article Fung says he revived "orthodox Chinese philosophy" in his earlier work and that this was a crime against China, as it had no part to play any more.
> "Orthodox philosophy," he continues, was the theoretical basis of feudal and landlord class rule in old China. Fung's books on this during the anti-Japanese period supposedly omitted the older philosophy bearing on the feudal system; some change in his views had already begun. But now he sees that this was not enough. The balance he then established was an old-system defense of concealed class-rule. Fung does not seem to show the process of his reasoning here, but he states the conclusions as factual. He lists the six books he had written and then describes his 1950 article examining his former thought: "Self-Criticism of New Moral Science." The key to his shift of position appears to be that Marxist-Leninist thought is practical, "materialist," and capable of solving problems of society and science, while logical analysis is really an idealistic approach not able to solve any practical problem — the tendencies of which were away from actualities to illusion. — From Peking *Kuang Ming Jih Pao*, October 26, 1952 — Summarized in *SCMP*, No. 452, November 14, 1952. Pp. 22-27.

A problem like Fung's is sobering at the very least. This man has a keen mind; he is presumably not under duress of actual force. As we shall see, it seems quite unlikely that the Communists used force with "intellectuals," and quite unlikely that they needed to use it. As we are approaching this whole range of phenomena from the standpoint of religious psychology it may not be necessary to breach this discussion to provide an explanation. It has been informally suggested that what may have happened to some Chinese in the present era is that they have discovered a new sense of history, a new historical metaphysic, so that their perspective has suddenly shifted and they have taken on new roles with respect to their newly-perceived destiny. The case of "Little Hsu" may help to show this in the situation of a young boy who is being worked on by his teachers and his peers.

Before coming to Little Hsu let the reader allow himself the small comic relief of an account of the newly-conscientious lives of college teachers who are being reconstructed under Communist ideology. It seems that college teachers must have wasted a great deal of time working too hard, and the commissars of education decided that the welfare of China demanded a change. The teachers must rest themselves more intelligently.

> "Tsing hua University Makes Continuous Progress in Arranging Time of Study, Work, and Rest for the Teachers and Students."

> "The Party Committee of Tsinghua University led and pushed the university in a great leap forward in all kinds of work ...

> "During the last ten days of May, the Party Committee of Tsinghua University adopted concrete measures and laid down rigid stipulations for enforcing the system of coordinating labor with rest ..." The day was to include 7 hours of rest, 8 hours of sleep, and 9 hours of study daily. It was stipulated that the time before 7 a.m., between 12:30 and 2:30 p.m., and after 9:30 p.m. should be used as time for rest and sleep; lights were to be out at 10 p.m. and everyone should "leave bed" at 6 a.m. The hours from 4:30-7 p.m. were to be free for doing personal business. There should be rest at noon. Teaching was to be in 3 units per week, morning, afternoon, and evening each being a unit. "All persons are to do whatever they like on Saturday evening and Sunday."
> —SCMP, No. 2339, Sept. 16, 1960. Pp. 7 & ff.

Well, it is easy to lampoon these things.

Notice the matter-of-fact position taken by Ma Hsü-lun, Minister of Higher Education, in an address to university authorities of North China on the policy and tasks of higher education. The conclusion runs:

> "Comrades: in order to make a success of higher education it behooves the Ministry of Higher Education to assume the

responsibilities of leadership, and it is for all the teachers and students of institutions of higher education to acquire the correct understanding, shoulder their responsibilities, and keep in step to work in unison. Only thus shall we be enabled to fulfill the glorious task entrusted to us by the nation.''
—SCMP, No. 576, May 22, 1953

This is on the blunt side as a statement of policy, but as a philosophy it may offer a clue to the nature of the relation between the individual and the Communist state. Clearly these people are under pressure from their version of the really-Real. The pressure may have mellowed as the bloom of the revolution grows older, and it may be a little more practical now than in its days of anxiety. Let us see how the psychological machinery works as shown in the case of Little Hsu. The account is from a magazine article:

"The Ideological Work of Young Communist
League Branches as Viewed from the
Progress Made by a Fellow Student."
—Shih Chi-K'uei

"When Little Hsu first joined the Foreign Languages school he gave one a bad impression. He came from a bourgeois family, and bourgeois ideas and mode of life had had a deep effect on him. He was not accustomed to sleeping on a wooden bed and eating coarse foods. He was indifferent to politics. He did not read newspapers for months. He was often the one with the poorest record in his class in current events. He led a liberalist life and took no part in collective activities. While his general records were satisfactory, he did not study hard and prided himself on being out of the ordinary. He used to sit in his dormitory listening to the radio while his fellow students were devoting themselves to study in their classroom. Once the school organized study of the documents of the 8th plenum of the 8th CCP Central Committee. Little Hsu, who seldom read newspapers, could not make out what was called 'the 8th plenum of the 8th CCP Central committee.' Secretary of the League branch Hu Chung-hua exhorted him to intensify the study of politics. Unexpectedly, Little Hsu shook his head and waved his hand, saying: 'I have no affinity with politics in this life. Leave it to the next world.' Was such a youth to be united with and given help? . . ."

Still, it was a YCL responsibility to help him, and Little Hsu really longed for socialism and was willing to be helped; so they decided to help him. His fellows began with questions of interest to him: to do a good professional job he would have to study politics, so he began to do this. The YCL branch had a great awakening; a person's internal combustion engine had first to be started, or outside force could do nothing.

But he still did this only for his job. The YCL chapter found that his family had doted on him, and the members worked on him to show him the bourgeois nature of his family, to make it clear that his family opposed what was best for him. He finally applied for membership in the League chapter, saying: "I must make a change. I want to be a good youth of the right type. I don't want to lag behind others in various fields. I want to give others a good impression. Joining the League I can become a good youth." The YCL replied: "But does it occur to you that if you want to join the League simply because you want to give others a good impression, you still have yourself in mind? If so, who will undertake the revolutionary cause of the world?" So now he began to see that before joining the League one must have a clear purpose of life, to fight for the communist ideal. This was the truth of life he must know.

—From *Chung-Kuo Ch'ing-nien.*
Summarized in *SCMM,*
No. 301, February 19, 1962. Pp. 8 and ff.

This passage is of great interest for the light it casts on some of the ways in which "conversions" may come about. If the account is reasonably accurate, and we can perhaps assume it is, several powerful factors were operating. The conviction of the large-group leaders was crucial; it was baffled, puzzled, and long-suffering, but it was constant. A Western church which could count on such steadfastness of idea and purpose would surely consider itself well served. Insight into the dynamics of the problem and immediate concern for its philosophic relations are present and effective in these Chinese situations. Commendable intelligence is clearly at work here, as well as moral conviction. As we know, the combination of positive factors operating on Little Hsu brought about a change in the boy's attitude. The operative elements are probably group influence toward establishment of a revised philosophic frame of reference, and the inducement of effort somewhat by resonance. Notice the element of extended patience on the part of the group leaders; a considerable period of time is involved in this episode.

In anybody's book this is a highly effective piece of proselyting work. From the western standpoint there is both laughter and tragedy in the minor drama contained in Little Hsu's story. Little Hsu himself is a threat to sobriety; he is so like some students we know that the description of him is irresistibly funny. The humor of the description is lost on the Chinese writers and on the original group leaders, but this is a deep fault in all of this literature; there is no humor in it anywhere. If nothing else were to cause Communism to founder in the course of time, Fagginger Auer used to say, its total lack of humor would surely do so.

From the western standpoint the casually negative attitude toward family life as represented in the emotional patterns of Little Hsu and the effective attack on them in the course of group-influence on this one lost sheep are difficult to respect, just as in a different dimension the elimination of the landlords was a social development difficult to comprehend and impossible to respect. In family life normal human emotions are not to be replaced by social-group programs, as in the social realm the elimination of social evil is hardly to be brought about in any lasting way by the stupid expedient of shooting it. The Communists will discover that evil will not be conquered in this way.

Still another episode, this time dealing with the adult psychology of involvement, demands inclusion in connection with the theme of religious psychology.

"Conquer Illness with the Firm Determination of a Revolutionary"

"Comrade Wang Kuan-lan, a deputy director of the Rural Work Dept. of the Central Committee of the Chinese Communist Party, suffered from a bad gastro-intestinal disease for 13 long years . . ." He was ill in the long march to Yenan; Mao Tse-Tung sent for him, told him to calm down, stay well, told him to learn to distinguish between what was important and what was not. "We want lazy men to learn to be diligent and diligent men to learn to be clever," said Mao. Wang was greatly moved by these words. But he didn't heed the advice; by 1941 he was ill again with insomnia, enteritis, and neurasthenia. In Yenan Central Hospital, Mao came to see him again, walking the 5 or 6 li of mountain path from Yangchialing . . . .

"Though I felt utterly exhausted after many sleepless days and nights, yet I was aroused as soon as I saw Chairman Mao enter. I looked at him as if he were my long-missed father or elder brother. He approached my bed in an easy and unhurried gait, and sitting down on a narrow hard bench in front of it, said comfortingly, "If you can't sleep, just lie there quietly. Don't try to rush yourself to sleep, and sleep will come.'' His kind concern and words greatly increased my power of fighting against my disease . . . . ''

At this point Wang showed a scroll in Mao's bold handwriting, and said it was his most valuable possession since it was with the strength it gave him that he had conquered his disease . . . . Here is what Mao wrote: ''Since it has come, you may as well take it easy. You don't have to fidget at all. Let your body slowly give rise to a power of resistance which will struggle against and finally defeat it. This is how one should deal with a chronic disease. Even if one has contracted an acute disease, one must let one's doctor deal with it and need not fidget oneself, for fidgeting will lead you nowhere. You must be firmly resolved to struggle against your disease, but you must not fidget. This is how I look at diseases. I record it for the information of Comrade Wang Kuan-lan.''

Wang Kuan-lan was very ill in several relapses afterward, but recovered; once he was in extremis, but declined to see his wife and children, feeling that the emotional experience would kill him. ''My condition being what it was, I absolutely could not afford any further exhaustion. I believed that I would be able to see my children again. Besides, as I was facing such a crisis my first obligation to the Party was to defeat my disease and death, not to see my wife or children . . . . And again, '' . . . If I died in this way would I not disappoint the Party and Chairman Mao?'' — ''To control myself I exercised the greatest will power. I set these rules for myself: not to look when I could not look, not to think when I could not think, not to move when I could not move, and not to speak when I could not speak . . . '' So he defeated hemorrhage, and in August 1946 was able to get up and begin again to walk. ''Later still I managed to walk from one room to another, from inside the hospital to outside, and from the plains up to the mountains. When I once more inhaled fresh mountain air, I could not help shouting aloud, ''It is the Party and Chairman Mao that have given me a new life.''

Later, as the region came under attack by Chiang Kai-Shek he was evacuated from Yenan. He had several minor relapses. In 1953 in Peking a gastrectomy took place with three-fourths of his stomach being removed; this effected a complete cure.

After the recital of this episode Comrade Wang Kuan-lan continued: ''How one should deal with one's disease is an important question. It is my understanding that if we have the firm revolutionary determination, place our diseased bodies in a completely objective position, control them and cooperate well with our doctors, we shall be able to expedite our recovery. If we show weakness in front of our diseases we shall not be able to defeat them. Many are the tests which the Party has for us revolutionaries. Whether or not we have the firm revolutionary determination can also be shown by our struggle against diseases. We should be able to stand the tests not only of revolutionary struggles of all kinds, but also of diseases. In such tests we must train ourselves and make ourselves stronger men."

—From *Chung-Kuo Ching-nien*, No. 4, February 16, 1961. Summarized in *SCMM*, No. 257, April 17, 1961. Pp. 31-36.

This account of Wang's illness is remarkable for several factors. Notice first the nature of the illness; it could well have had a nervous origin or component so that the episode is set up from the first as a profound internal conflict of the self-will of the believer with the grace of the ultimate, salvation being the prize which is at stake. Notice too the visitation of Chairman Mao; one can refrain from describing it as theophany, but it is at the very least a manifestation of the prophet. The self-will of the communicant, however, still prevents his full absorption in the Reality of Communism. The Prophet then speaks and Wang receives his message on the earthy problem of the moment.

There follows an unusual display of self-discipline. There can be no denying the psychological reality of Wang's religious involvement; it becomes a profound religious experience. And yet, years later when the end of the story is told, after all the religious comings and goings are long past and Wang has been to the hospital at Peking for a three-quarter gastrectomy, the final comment has the sharpness of religious comedy, and the likeliest reaction is a Kierkegaardian guffaw. When all was said and done Wang Kuan-lan had a screwball stomach; this was the region where his light was spent.

Similar instances could be added indefinitely, as for example the phenomenon of the reception of redeemed sinners into the fold (*SCMP*, No. 2384, November 25, 1960: "Decree on Special Pardons") and numerous instances of the application of such legal redemptions (*SCMP*, No. 2153, December 10, 1959). There is the recurrent problem of the fall from grace by deliberate corruption or by simple failure to achieve perfection as shown by material results (*SCMP*, No. 557, April 24, 1953; "Shantung's Struggle Against Bureaucratism, Commandism, and Breaching of Law and Discipline." Commandism is a delightful term meaning the giving of too many orders, a remarkable insight for Communism to have had. One would cherish knowing whether the term is original or the contribution of a translator.) These readings are really delightful and filled with charm; they sometimes convey tragedy, but where the average citizen is involved they also convey a simple and childlike earnestness.

One remembers the fascinating juxtaposition of different emphases in the dimension of filial piety, indicating some mellowing from the doctrinaire rigidity of the early 1950's to a wiser position made clear as early as 1954, which for ideological development is practically breakneck speed and must of course represent a formal change of policy. There is such a comparison in Karl Eskelund, *The Red Mandarins,* 1959, Chapter IX, where Lao Ma, the "Old Horse," recounts the accusation of Yao by his returned son, Tai Cheng, and another in the quite different story and attached commentary to be found in *SCMP,* No. 973, January 21, 1955, pp. 29-32, where filial piety is pronounced good and official as long as it is not specifically counter-revolutionary.

A number of dramatic tales could often represent potentially high drama, and actively invite the reader to critical, psychological and philosophic examination. For a taste of such drama there is a brief and scornful story entitled "What Happened on the Banks of the Shum-Chun River" (*SCMP,* No. 2374, November 8, 1960). Again one would like to know if the dramatic qualities of story and diction are those of the original writer or of the translator. Surely these stories are evidence that great intensity of emotional commitment is engendered on both sides of contemporary Mainland Chinese political questions. In this period China was not yet at peace.

One concluding comment, however, should perhaps be made, for its own sake and for its possible bearing on the issue of apparent religious themes in recent Chinese thought. It does appear that the metaphysics of Communism in China is different in kind from the metaphysics of Communism in the West. Some evidences suggest that Ultimate Reality for Chinese Communism does not lie in the field of economics and economic forces, as is the case in Western Communist theory, but rather in the field of politics and political forces. Consider for example *SCMP,* No. 560, April 29, 1953: "China Democratic League's Participation in National Cultural-Educational Activities." Also less precisely, *SCMM,* No. 300, February 12, 1962, Chang Shih-ying on "Truth Is Concrete," an entertaining discussion of proper intellectual process, incidentally containing two funny stories illustrating nonconcreteness in thinking. One is the story of Sun Pin's strategy against the Wei troops, and the other is allegedly by Hegel, on the way to generalize on the subject of stinking eggs. Someone had better prove that Hegel really wrote this.

If it should in fact be the case that the Chinese Communist ultimate lies in the field of politics, it might suggest that Chinese Communist thought is more nearly indigenous to Chinese culture than has been thought, and that the relation of Peking to Moscow is more a matter of convenience than either a genuine philosophic alliance or a dependence. It might also be that contemporary Mainland Chinese themes express old Chinese Confucian concerns far more than they represent recent Western political motifs, and perhaps because of the amazing intensity of the moral demands made upon the individual, that they may tend to represent a throwback to classical or ancient Confucianism, when there was almost nothing extant except the moral imperative in the midst of chaos, rather than simply a re-expression of neo-Confucian themes of merely six hundred years ago. It may be that if a typing of the Communist reversion were to be made, it would be well to wait and see whether the gathering re-assertion of ceremonial civilization turns out to be pervasive. If it should, then we would expect the reassertion of old China which may be represented in Chinese Communism to be neo-Confucian rather than classically Confucian, and to be that much more transitory as a cultural phenomenon. This question like others should not be pressed too far, and must remain open for the time being.

XII The Chariot-Wheels of King Milinda; Comparative Notions of the Ultimate

In our enlightened and modern age, when so many difficult matters are at last so very clearly understood and when so many mysteries have been displaced by antiseptic chromium with electronic controls, it is sobering to find in a single class of twenty college students as many living instances of nearly all the major philosophical positions of the last 600 years. Every college teacher in a reflective field has had the experience of suddenly realizing that he confronts in some unaware student a throwback to the muddy dreads of a 16th-century Protestantism, to a 17th-century antinomianism of an American variety with its fateful insistence on individual interpretation of religious truth, to a 19th-century transcendentalism wandering headily among the stars on moonless nights, or to some similar phenomenon of different vintage. And if this comment seems to overlook the glassy stare of 18th-century rationalism it is only because religious liberals of two centuries later, among whom some of us are numbered, present so acute a resemblance to the little rubber clowns that children play with in the summertime, the ones with weights in their feet so that no matter how they are tipped release returns them instantly to their former stance. Do economists, sociologists or teachers of English literature find in their fields, too, parallels to the old belief of biologists that the life-history of the species was subsumed in the development of the individual life-unit? Certainly there are times when the teacher of a reflective study feels himself in the presence of an organism which is breathing philosophic bubbles through little fish-gills where no gills ought to be, happily ignorant of the bizarre appearance of his activity, eventually departing waggle-tail, waggle-tail out the office door, leaving a double trail of airy circles and under-water sound-effects which regrettably cannot be reproduced at this time.

This is simply to say that an enormous variety of reflective ideas are vividly personified in any aggregation of living persons at particular times, and that by no means all of these ideas are mutually contemporary or close to it. A teacher can find a de facto positivist, aged 17½ and convinced apparently beyond possibility of redemption, sitting in his class two points off the port rostrum, but he can as readily find a Platonist, a 15th century devotee of Whitehead's "brute fact," one of a variety of mystics, a practicing disciple of the Black Arts, or a sentimental animist or two. The reverse should also be the case: much older ideas should as readily reflect more 'modern' views, and of course as in Theravada Buddhism this is indeed so. This is also to point out the one-to-one articulation of person and idea as a fact of common experience. To encounter the philosopher, even the inadvertent philosopher of tender years, is to grapple with a system, specificated or merely implied, and to be able to study it at first hand in the form it takes when given life beyond the printed page. Ideas afoot with life are after all the natural composition of philosophies; the printed page is the abstraction, difficult though it may be to remember. What is to be learned from this about the nature and use of reflective systems?

Ultimates in Theravada Buddhism

To put philosophic system into the form of individual human life is perhaps to make more obvious what is certainly the case anyway—the fact that each system must have a foundation from which to depart on its constructional round, and that each must also have at least a shadowed conception of ultimate reality from which to depend its pattern of interlocked relations. Some systems have a God, some an elegant first principal, some a substance, a process, or a law. There has to be a foundation, and there has to be an ultimate. These appear to be not always the same thing, although there would be a natural tendency for them to coincide.

It is convenient to treat even a printed philosophic system like a well-intentioned college student, and to ask it questions designed to let it show how it arrived at those of its conclusions which are of major interest to it. What questions may one ask?

Surely, the triad which come to mind would go far toward establishing a clear relation between individual and universe. These would be first the question which serves as the focus of this sketch: "What is the nature of the real, or the ultimate?" and thereafter two questions which for the moment are secondary but which might well be primary: "What is the nature of the self, or of human nature?" and "How does man know what he says he knows?" The middle question is of course a prime concern of Buddhism, and the last is a question which the plethora of dimensions and continua in modern times has made it necessary to ask in almost every connection, whereas in former times it would have been largely superfluous or perhaps an interesting exercise. To initiate a brief series of instances it may be well to ask of Theravada Buddhism what it means by what it says about the really real.

In the extended conversation held by King Milinda with the venerable Nagasena to decide whether there is a self or Ego, or more generally, to see whether an entity can be said to exist on the grounds that parts of it exist, and that the whole must be more than the aggregate of parts, the conclusion is reached that there is no self or Ego. Nagasena asks how King Milinda travelled when he came to visit him: did he walk or ride? King Milinda replies that he came by chariot, whereupon Nagasena, in an exchange which could have served as an example for Socrates to follow, proceeds to take the chariot apart piece by piece and to insist that the king tell him whether the chariot was contained in the pole, or the axle, the wheels, or any of its other parts. The king responds obediently in the exchange and the conclusion is reached that the entity cannot be accounted for in any of its parts. Therefore there is no chariot. "The word chariot is a mere empty sound. The word 'chariot' is but a way of counting, term, appellation, convenient designation, and name for pole, axle, wheels, chariot-body, and banner-staff." The same question is raised in other connections.

Now quite clearly the issue is whether universals exist or whether they do not, and equally clearly, whether one finds the conclusion or its method sound will be a function of what one's prior decision on the existence of universals has been. There is no blinking this difficulty. Nagasena simply asked the wrong questions, or more accurately, he refrained from asking the right question, which would have been—not allowing for his Socratic privilege of bending the query his way—"Does not the totality of the parts of the chariot comprise the chariot?" King Milinda, by this time well trained as a philosophic straight-man, would have promptly answered, "Yes," and the entire subsequent history of Buddhism would have been different.

Philosophers are human and they have their preferences. Some like spinach and some do not, and there is no accounting for taste, intellectual or gustatory. The facts are that Theravada Buddhism took the position that universals do not exist, and apparently it resolved to prove it by not mentioning the matter for 2,000 years. It seems hardly cricket for us to raise the issue at this point; if we do so it will be merely as part of an effort to understand Theravada Buddhism and not at all with any suggestion that classic Buddhism should modify its stand against the gossamer grounds of particular being.

To be more specific, notice that Theravada Buddhism takes this position even while it maintains an epistemology which is radically assertive in certain respects. For an academic psychologist in a Western institution to advance a pattern of human nature as detailed and as self-assured as the Buddhist analysis of consciousness, for example, would cause howls of professional anguish among his colleagues who might feel that the pyramidal masonry of mental awareness had hardly been documented to such a precise degree.

Here the Buddhist says he knows, while the Western social scientist says he does not know. The Buddhist, of course, howls in his turn when it is suggested that the whole is more than the sum of its parts, because, you see, this hasn't been properly proved. As William Ellery Leonard abruptly remarked in a different connection long ago, "so much depends on the point of view." To be sure, all knowledge is assertive, which is to say that it is broadly conceptual in its nature, but a good many epistemologists seem to be without this important awareness, and it is certainly unfair to make unusual demands on classical Buddhism in this regard. The assertive or conceptual nature of knowing means to convey a nearly substantive epistemological relation between subject and object. That is, subject to the usual failure of language to provide vehicles for reflection, the reference is to the full range of relation between subject and object, including the essential identity of subject and object, the essential dependence of each upon the other, the essentially creative or creational, and essentially sustaining, nature of knowledge.

Granted the selective nature of Buddhist epistemology, it remains to ask what is the nature of Buddhist reality. Here again it depends which way one looks. To direct the examining gaze inward among the walls and corridors of selfhood is to discover a labyrinthine structure of mind and matter, the justification for which is no doubt held to be experiential. This basis for certainty involves a considerable expansion of the empirical dimension; in some form reflective philosophies all do resort to interpretations of the content of experience. How dull the world of the West if this were not so! What would one do with the world-views of Reinhold Niebuhr, Seelye Bixler, Martin Buber, Paul Tillich, and all the others, if their referrals for ultimate evidence to the experience of the human self were not to be honored. In accordance with the epistemological position taken earlier, the remark refers equally to all major reflective positions, to those of A. J. Ayer and Charles Stevenson, for example, whose theories of human nature would have very little in them in the way of substantive content but would be of equal significance in their total systems for all that, and so to a deceptive system such as that of Sartre in *Being and Nothingness,* in which the vivid impression of a philosophic horseman moving at full gallop is marred only by the suspicion that he has no head. This is why the issue of the definition of human nature is one of the fundamental triad of questions to be asked about any world-view. It is as impossible for a reflective system to exist without a notion of the self as it is for one to exist without a conception of objective reality, or without the epistemological connection.

Gazing now outward among supposedly external objects, we may make bold to ask what the Buddhist natural universe is like, what its degree of reality is, and whether there is anywhere in its pattern room or function for a notion of the ultimate. These questions reduce to one question and are answered in one answer.

Buddhism denies the notion of an ultimate, but we will perhaps be forgiven for observing that people do this much of the time and all it ever means is that cultural attention is simply being directed elsewhere. Buddhism knows what its ultimate units are—the axle, pole, and wheels of King Milinda's chariot—and it would have us believe that these are all there is. Supposing this were the case and these really are all there is, then the Buddhist notion of the ultimate becomes simply the vast revolving ball of seething units and events, the numberless bleak "point-instants," in Malalasekera's happy term, which make up the only substance which the universe can be said to have, weaving in and out among each other's spaces, related only by the constructs imposed upon them by human aggregates of other point-instants which in turn have no color of their own as aggregates, but are merely the illusory self-ascriptions of color on a basis defined as non-existent.

A "western" reservation must be entered at this point. There is a Kierkegaardian language-problem in a discussion of this character, the kind of problem which arises when there really are no proper words for what one means to say, and when the terms one is compelled to use because a given language holds no others of any greater usefulness only serve to misdirect the reader well beside the mark. The content of such fundamental Buddhist concepts as suffering, being, and elements of existence, might perhaps be examined, although in suggesting it, one is at once aware that more than twenty centuries of study have gone into just these concepts, on the part of scholars who have had some claim to know what the terms originally conveyed. But there is fortunately no end to learning, perhaps because the constant evolution of new conditions, gyrations of the seething ball, compel new alignments and require reconstruction and re-description of existing relations of subject and object, which is what knowledge is when you come to think of it.

One is inclined to restate every so often that the swiftly changing intercultural situation of mid-20th century, marked chiefly by accelerated speed of communication, places mankind in a situation which is simply without precedent. It is no longer exclusively the business of an individual or a group what major conceptual position is held in the privacy of mind or in the relatively public formulations of general agreement. The traditional American right of private opinion and judgment may remain inviolate, and it is not intended to attack that principle. It is intended to point out that in the developing situation of contemporary times an influence such as that of Henry Thoreau on Mahatma Gandhi, and through Gandhi on Indian culture and on cultures which take their cue from India, may no longer take ninety years to happen, or seventy, or even fifty. The effects may be felt with lightning speed, and the consequences may involve life or death for millions of persons. Therefore it is reasonable to look for new conceptual understandings of Buddhist thought, not only for their own sake and value but also because Buddhist Burma is scarcely a day's journey from New England, and less by wire; because a distinguished Burmese gentleman of great ability has presided over the United Nations in a position of unparalleled power and influence; and because in the inexorable evolution of cultural affairs the world of next week or next month is likely to become an Asiatic world rather than to continue to be a Western world, and might just possibly be the better for it. If there is even the smallest chance that the Buddhist-Christian relation can be subsumed more effectively at some present moment than has been done before, surely the effort is well required of us. On identical grounds it would be the present view that the relation between Protestantism and Catholicism in the West should be radically rethought. Conceivably the Atlantic community is approaching the end of the values of the Protestant schism, those remaining to it being associated with individualistic habits of thought, a place for which should be sculptured into an enduring cathedral of heart and mind. So let it be noted that in one interpretation what classical Buddhism has done is to shift the function of conceived Divinity from external Personality to substantive Process, to generalize the idea of substance itself from the level of inference to the level of specification. A Westerner less concerned to deny ideas such as that of Divinity would incline to consider classical Buddhism as a pan-Deism, operating on a hollowed-out Kantian psychology from which the function of reason is largely removed, and terminating somewhere near a restricted Kantian idealism. A comment of this type is of help only in indicating that there very probably are regions of contact, perhaps of partial identity, among reflective positions of diverse natures. The conclusion would be that Theravada Buddhism has a notion of an ultimate fully as relevant as that of any system, and more explicit than most; active, functional, and in plain sight, in fact so thoroughly in the public domain that one can hardly refer to it without breaking one's foot.

The Ultimate in St. Thomas

The writings of St. Thomas, especially the *Summa Theologica,* I, 1-26, 75-102, and II, 90-108, whatever else they may be, are an exercise in the trust of reason as a faculty of mind and a means to knowledge, and this being so, they are read today with even a sense of melancholy. It would be pleasant and reassuring if we could think that the faculty of reason made a difference in the general metaphysics of men. It finds common use, to be sure, on numerous small scales as a tool of investigation and short-run extrapolations of little moment. This is, however, not a time in which the special gift and genius of Western culture is first called upon or perhaps even finally resorted to for definitive structuring of the grounds of existence, human nature, and the relation of subject and object. The vacuum is of course temporary and the melancholy therefore unnecessary. Cultural adventuring such as the existential philosophies of recent times and the bizarre positivisms of scientific back-alleys have ways of working themselves out. They reflect human capacities and possibilities, and their recurrences in a variety of forms are simply useful ways of getting them examined and judged in the market place of human endeavor. Reason, however, represents a capacity for cutting across lines and constructing communications among widely different sets of cultural phenomena, so that one may reserve the right to regret that it does not find full usefulness at a time when its functions are in great demand.

But to get on with the business, in Question 2, Article 3, paragraph 6 of his *Summa Theologica,* Aquinas speaks of the end of causal regression in a first cause:

> But this cannot go on to infinity, because then there would be no first mover, and, consequently, no other mover . . . . Therefore it is necessary to arrive at a first mover which is moved by no other. And this everyone understands to be God.

The same argument is varied only a little in the next three paragraphs, and slightly more in the last. On what grounds then does St. Thomas assert the existence of God? On the ground that if one circumstance obtains, another, the next, is necessary. What "everyone understands" is incidental; the essential connection is logical necessity.

This is an interesting change for a late-Protestant mind-set to encompass. How would a contemporary non-Thomist religious philosopher establish grounds for a similar resolution of the issue? Very likely by placing the emphasis on the last sentence—"And this everyone understands to be God"—for the common feeling and experience of men tends to be the final court of appeal in the quest for religious evidence in the non-rationalist mood which derives from Kierkegaard and his followers.

The decided genius of Aristotelian Thomism lies precisely here, that it was able to move from a Platonist, idealist rationalism to a realism which allowed for constant immersion in the objective world of things and objects, knowledge of which was to be had through sense, and thereby threw open to the questing human mind the endless vistas and perspectives which follow on recognition of the complex of levels and depths of sensory awareness, as when in the changing lights of late-afternoon one looks out new windows on the west to study the moving shadows on the hills, their subtleties of shape and shade and motion, seeing a hundred different versions of the real in less than a hundred minutes, each one there for the perceiving, each one representing a depth relation as real or as objective as all the rest, the entire succession serving to remind one of the fundamental relation of subject and object without which existence is a warped misconception and human nature without a half of being.

Therefore Thomism as a philosophy was modern before modern times were thought of; if recent revaluations of the late medieval period have altered its configuration with early medieval and early Renaissance times, articulating the three periods so that the achievements of St. Thomas represent a radical alteration of the grounds of epistemological relation and so of metaphysics in the most general sense, the Thomistic accomplishment is then not merely the classic medieval "synthesis" which breaks down with the work of Bacon and his successors, the Italian Renaissance, and the so-called scientific revolution of the sixteenth and seventeenth centuries, but is quite clearly the precursor and enabler of the Renaissance and of the seemingly emancipated moods of modern times. Not to recognize this is to live in a hard provincialism bound—so to speak—hand and foot by as grim a set of partial concepts as ever we once thought were properly descriptive of the Middle Age. To this issue we will return in the passage on humanisms of recent stripe.

To present St. Thomas' descriptions of the characteristics of Divinity, from the Treatises on God, the Trinity, the Creation, and Man would not greatly enlarge the present point. In connection with the establishment of reason as a means toward comprehension of the nature of God, giving way to faith only in those farthest reaches of understanding where reason cannot go, much as the contemporary scientist literally does not know beyond a certain point whether he is encountering a wave or a particle and so must proceed operationally on a kind of faith, leaning far out to windward over the water simply to keep his function afloat at all, one may remark that the multifaceted conceptions of Divinity characteristic of Thomism are a result of its simultaneous conceiving of God as Person and as First Principle. Thus the peculiarly human capacity to understand ideas of enormous compass in poignant, human and dramatic terms is fully honored, while the equally human power of grasping reality intellectually is equally expressed in the dimension of God as first principle. Beyond both of these stands the realm of faith, defining the psychology of the closer approach to Divinity.

The Kierkegaardian Ultimate

In the catalogue of philosophic reflections of human capacities and human interests, Kierkegaard represents something quite different from systematic Western Christianity, and yet it is from him that the twin lines of existential psychology, religious and secular, derive, lines which appear to be by implication nearly as systematic, or soon to become so, as the Hegelian edifice against which Kierkegaard railed for most of his professional life. To resolve the particular question of interest to us here, there can hardly be any question as to Kierkegaard's holding of a notion of the ultimate. There can be a good deal of question as to the nature of God for Kierkegaard, but the fact that the question is unanswerable except by indirection is of the very genius of Kierkegaard's contribution to religious thought. Not alone by definition is God infinite and the Creator, but also by faith as distinct from reason, and only by faith among the various channels to awareness. Only when reason is set aside is the reality of God open to the prehension of faith.

At every point where the issue is raised, Kierkegaard turns against system, sometimes slurring Hegel in brief sarcasms in the novellas or attacking him by direct reference in the philosophic writings, and sometimes by general assault on the idea and method of system. A highly significant psychology is at the root of this view: reason has its uses, but it is to be abandoned where knowledge of God is at issue. The religious condition, a realm apart from the aesthetic and the ethical, involves a life and method apart from those of the other realms. In the *Concluding Unscientific Postscript,* he writes:

> The systematic Idea is the identity of subject and object, the unity of thought and being. Existence, on the other hand, is their separation. It does not by any means follow that existence is thoughtless; but it has brought about, and brings about, a separation between subject and object, thought and being. In the objective sense, thought is understood as pure thought; this corresponds in an equally abstract-objective sense to its object,

which object is therefore the thought itself, and the truth becomes the correspondence of thought with itself....

The existing subject on the other hand, is engaged in existing, which is indeed the case with every human being. Let us therefore not deal unjustly with the objective tendency, by calling it an ungodly and pantheistic self-deification; but let us rather view it as an essay in the comical. For the notion that from now on until the end of the world nothing could be said except what proposed a further improvement in an almost completed system, is merely a systematic consequence for systematists.

Now Kierkegaard was bright enough to know in general that systems do not work this way. At least they do not endure in the yellow-leaf condition in which he envisions them. They either disappear or they are reconstructed to take account of new conditions. Kierkegaard, however, is pursuing his usual course of speaking from an absolute position, juxtaposing the ideal and the actual, the infinite and the finite to reveal the absurdity of the relation and so pass a judgment of ridicule on the human situation.

Notice that Kierkegaard by his overstatement obscures his inability to separate himself completely from Christian realism. He too has a use for reason, and he apparently did not intend to allow his dethronement of the aesthetic to interfere substantially with his pragmatic adjustments. It did interfere, perhaps even substantially, but probably not much beyond that. His younger relatives remembered all their lives the captivating parties he gave for them and the joyful style of his doing so. Numerous stories have survived concerning his expensive and highly precise habits of life. He was never immoral as the world understands the term, but for a Kierkegaard as for an Augustine, small imperfections loom larger than for the rest of men.

What Kierkegaard essentially does is to create ways of contrasting by artistic means the realm of finite with the realm of the infinite, and to make inevitable the judgment of the former in terms of the latter. Curiously enough, this is not so difficult to do as one might think. Some of Kierkegaard's effectiveness as a religious thinker probably stems from a feeling which is common today that Kierkegaard achieved a profundity of insight into the truth and into the psychology of human approach to the truth which had rarely been duplicated before and never since. Kierkegaard's depth of insight was indeed profound, and as a literary preacher his effectiveness was enormous and well-deserved. His stature is hardly at issue. But the calling into question of the realm of the finite in terms of a flashing insight into the realm of the infinite probably happens every day, and within the experience of most of us at that.

It will be clear from those parts of the foregoing which are relevant to the issue that Kierkegaard's method was to sharpen a psychology of feeling, map it, and on the basis of its major features, suggest the implications for the Ultimate. Primarily Kierkegaard is a religious psychologist, and a Christian religious psychologist to boot. *The Attack Upon Christendom* is after all just one of those absolute judgments; it does not mean that Kierkegaard was not a Christian, or even that he was really angry at Bishop Mynster and Pastor Martensen. He probably had great respect for Bishop Mynster, and if we recall correctly he had quite other reasons for annoyance with Pastor Martensen. All that is conveyed by *The Attack Upon Christendom* is that when one makes an absolute judgment from the realm of the infinite upon some part of the realm of the finite this is the kind of result one gets.

Kierkegaard's means to religious awareness is especially clear in *The Concept of Dread* and related passages. It is as if the human sense of Angst with which the self comes unavoidably equipped, so to speak, by reason of its awareness of its perilous place in existence and its separation from God, were a chief means by which Kierkegaard suggests the awful power and majesty of God. It is as if Kierkegaard were a religious operationalist, and as a matter of fact, one may reasonably conclude that he was.

It is convenient to consider Kierkegaard's notion of the Ultimate and his ways of approach to the Ultimate because he is to a large degree an epitome of the Protestant mood and mind. He was a product of the Western Christian tradition in so many ways, and yet he lived his professional life in tension with the Lutheran Church of his day. He has a whole-souled respect for and devotion to the Christian God, and yet he must condemn all approaches to Divinity except his own; in the end he cannot abide even his own Church. He insists on an extreme individualism in religious experience and in the expression of religious truth, and yet when he writes of his religious insights he must appeal first to his own personal experience and beyond this to the experience of all men—and it is precisely the religious experience of other men which recognizes the degree of truth in Kierkegaard's judgment and its relevance in a social sense. Kierkegaard of course had no use for the judgments of the multitude. In one dimension there was an amazing arrogance, in another a profound humility. These are typically Protestant and typically prophetic qualities. Kierkegaard was both Protestant and prophet, and was no doubt among the greatest of each. He must represent within himself the gift which the Protestant mind at its best can make to the religious development of the West, and at the same time the hazards of having gifts so highly charged bestowed from so convinced a soul.

Humanistic Ultimates

It is a relief to return to some viewpoints which are not as diverting and as full of enticing by-ways as the ones just discussed, but it is not so easy to settle which humanists to choose for present purposes. Lord Russell turns out to be English, Kahlil Gibran to be Lebanese, and many philosophers of science working in America today to be of European extraction. This might not matter if we could find in them expression of some of the peculiarly American moods of recent times. It is a great temptation to choose an American and a Vermonter, Sylvia Hortense Bliss of Calais and Rochester, whose two slender volumes of prose-poems, *Quests* and *Sea Level,* privately printed in the 1920's and 1930's, are supplemented by re-issues and by a number of her published and unpublished philosophical studies of the nature and place of man in the new world of science. All of her work is available and appropriate, but to put the matter directly, the impeccably courteous but formidable Miss Bliss, who died in 1963 at the age of ninety-two, just wouldn't have liked it very well, and for all that philosophic discourse is free one who knew her well would not hasten to take the liberties of criticism and judgment with her ideas. This challenging task will be undertaken more appropriately after the passage of a longer time.

It has been unkindly remarked that most American humanists today are elder statesmen with the accent on elder. The humanist school can take comfort in this respect from Theravada Buddhism, the great age of which seems only to contribute to its perennial vigor. Let us therefore be content with two elder statesmen of our time, the familiar figure of another Vermonter, John Dewey, whose many-sided work can be discussed from almost any standpoint and who wouldn't have minded our discussing him since there is ample precedent for it, and the interesting figure of Johannes Abraham Christoffel Fagginger Auer, sometime Parkman Professor of Church History and Systematic Theology at the Harvard Divinity School, a native of the Netherlands on whose lapel gleamed the Order of Orange-Nassau but whose work is as American as Montpelier crackers.

To consider the two somewhat in concert, Dewey's theory of valuation is heavily social, that is, it hinges on the attitudes of people, and his discussion of the idea of God shows that this notion is in turn heavily dependent on the values held by people. God for Dewey is variously described as "a unification of ideal values that is essentially imaginative in origin when the imagination supervenes in conduct" and "the *active* relation between ideal and actual." Dewey does not insist that the term "God" be applied to this relation, but he personally thinks it would be useful to apply it because of the emotional affect which gathers around the name and the increased social efficiency which would result from a harnessing of the emotional energy to constructive social ends.

It is very like Dewey and not unlike some other people whom we all know that he should have wanted to be efficient about God. It really was not irreverent, nor was that letter irreverent which one remembers so vivdly from an inveterate and unreconstructed industrial engineer who remarked in connection with a social survey of the liberal church that what religious liberals needed was a series of practical ways to increase God's output. One wonders what God would have thought of that observation, typical as it is of the pragmatic American who feels that all problems are solvable in sensible ways if people with good intentions will just get on with the job. The divine judgment passed on the engineer would have been far gentler than the judgments passed by some of the Lord's lieutenants on earth. Some of the sharper neo-orthodox comments on the aging Protestant liberalism of a generation ago come to mind in this connection. More kindly ways of exchanging ideas ought to be invented.

To look momentarily for Dewey's self-subsisting entity as a means of filling out his system, it can only be found in the social and cultural aggregate, the enormous welter of milling humanity from which so large a part of individual education derives in the form of communicational experience of complex kinds. This is Dewey's metaphysic. Much of his attention has to do with working out ways of operating practically and efficiently in a methodological dimension of experiment within the framework of a social metaphysic. Beyond this he does not ask the question, as Theravada Buddhism also prefers simply not to concern itself with questions called speculative.

The reflective commentator must of course be permitted his little mischief: he wants to know what happens when you ask the question anyhow. Quite clearly what happens is that one gets one of those revolving-ball systems of metaphysics in which everything depends on what happens next door, nothing precedes or follows anything, and the only way to describe its notion of the ultimate is to look for that which endures and to which subsidiary questions are referred. In Dewey's system this is the social value, man in his social dimension, dynamic society. To the question of the "class paradox" raised in Herbert McArthur's study, "Metasemantics East and West," Dewey has no answer. His ultimate reality must feed on itself, hoping that no one will raise the issue of its proper nourishment.

Fagginger Auer functioned in the same league, but as Helen Coffee used to say, he was "a horse from another garage." He was a metaphysician deprived of his raw materials, a born commander of philosophic troops whose logistics had suffered an interruption. He was forever talking about proving something when there wasn't anything to prove, and he pretended to be quite regretful about it. As a matter of fact one suspects that he actually did regret it, but unfortunately that is the way the world wags. In *Humanism States Its Case* he wrote:

> Granted the existence of a God, wise enough and powerful enough to cause all things to work together for ultimate good, no difficulty worth mentioning is left. We simply entrust to this God the care of all things, notably the care for the moral education of man. God explains to man the meaning and importance of his plans and likewise the need for living in accordance with the eternal laws through which those plans are slowly developed and realized. Man recognizes this need and without further question accepts the rules of behavior by which God desires that he should regulate his actions. The moral problem is solved; there is no plan to be discovered anywhere.

At this point Professor Auer had his tongue so far into his cheek that he could hardly talk.

Humanism quite agrees (he continued) that there is no flaw in the logic anywhere. But the whole matter is conditioned upon the actual existence of a God who directs our motions, which is the very question at issue. We are not allowed to reason from the desirability of a condition to the existence of that condition. This would be to repeat the mistake which St. Anselm made in connection with the ontological argument. We may believe in the existence of a God if we wish; there is no law against it, but we cannot prove the fact.

Here is a logician tipping his hand, a rationalist railing against the Platonists, a scholastic in apparent misery because he has no proof of final things. But Professor Auer had an answer for his own predicament. He would withdraw the ultimate question, resolving firmly to be content with what can be proved and what is left. Auer meant scientific proof, of course, and this raises the issue of the nature of scientific knowledge.

Auer's residual reality, if it is pressed to show itself at a given moment, must be another of the revolving-ball systems, centering around man as Dewey's system does, but with a difference. Auer, while he was determined to be hard-boiled and to write off the entire realm of the scientifically unprovable at least until new and provable discoveries brought better days, was still a rationalist trafficking in the coin of the rationalist realm. He sounds like an Aquinas who has forgotten his reading notes, and in his implied conveyance of what the nature of God would be if there were a nature of God he sounds not a little like Kierkegaard reaching for the wholly other. Kierkegaard's subjectivism does not appear, but the order of discourse is oddly similar.

Initial Conceptualism

It will perhaps be clear that these critiques are written from a base, and that the direction is toward a constructionist or conceptualist epistemology. That is, with each philosophic system or world-view there is a metaphysical outreach from the central self, however that may be described, into the surrounding universe; the type of outreach may vary as schools or reflective positions vary, but the effect is the same. The individual self is thus responsible for selecting, constructing and maintaining its own world. Communication is real and effective, and the place of process is not in doubt.

This form of substantive connection between subject and object requires that the fundamental conceptual process be identical for all viewpoints and types of metaphysics, that the process of knowing be one process for all epistemological efforts, for science and religion, for rationalisms and humanisms, for idealisms and existentialisms. Epistemology then becomes a projective function of the personality, taking many forms as cultural or individual interests may direct, and finding in the objective hinterlands responding forms from which subject-object configurations are constructed.

From this standpoint, systems which are apparently diverse come to be less greatly dissimilar, and the processes from which they result become of primary interest. Each of these four religious philosophies reflects a set of capacities of the human self as well as a set of characteristics of the objective universe. They come from very different periods in the history of thought; other systems might have been selected from still other periods with similar patterns emerging. The point to be made may have more to do with the ways in which thought-systems behave than with internal contents of the systems. A major burden of modern times may be to learn to use thought-systems as instruments for the widening and deepening of knowledge of man and universe, this in place of the ancient tendency of men to become victims of their views of truth, to propel themselves into oppositions or warfares because of differences of world-view. To do this one must deal in commonalities of widely divergent thought-systems, being willing to generalize far enough to disclose common characteristics in seemingly polarized nexi. Time factors may be insignificant in useful comparisons of the great ways of thought. Perhaps the little intellectual fish-gills which a teacher sees breathing and bubbling in his college classrooms, all unaware of their anachronistic oddity in the history of thought, are more nearly to a useful point than the devoted schoolman would have guessed, let him be realist, positivist, rationalist, existentialist, or what he will.

XIII The Arrow and the Song: A Note on the Metaphysics of History

To the New Englander whose life is set among the tall steeples of Unitarianism the moment of church union with the Universalists allowed review of a thesis on the meaning of historical derivation of liberal religious principles.

Ideas and reflective positions do not appear to age in a single direction as other things do. They may indeed grow old, and they surely change. But they can also grow young again and even be re-born in some new form. The clergyman and the teacher frequently encounter in living persons sets of ideas which belong somewhere else in time. A minister may know quite well that he is addressing on a Sunday morning a congregation containing some Lockeian of Humeian empiricists from the eighteenth century, several nineteenth century evolutionists, a few twentieth century positivists or existentialists (who may very well be throwbacks to an earlier time), and some timeless mystics who cannot be bothered with systems or centuries at all. The teacher of philosophy or of religion is occasionally aware that he has among his students a remarkable collection of archaic and contemporary viewpoints, all defending themselves vigorously and attacking their opponents brightly, not caring that their positions may have been modified for excellent reasons several centuries ago or happily unthinking that their ultra-modern notions may not hold water longer than another ten years. This is not to set ministers and teachers apart; it is merely to suggest that time is not the same for ideas as for mountains or buildings of biological life-units. In a sense the reflective person lives in many ages at once, and he must be aware of it if he intends to meet his challenges.

The thesis is that historical connections among derivative points of view are seldom if ever lost, that original meanings continue to inhere in later modifications or reformulations of earlier positions, and that continuous metaphysical threads can be said to tie together the systems of yesterday with those of today and those of tomorrow.

What is so odd about this? Do we not always trace the threads of connection among periods and points of view, showing how one has come from another, and how they are similar and how different? We do, but beyond the study and the writing of history a different attitude may be taken toward the nature of the real as represented in history.

Notice that this is a comment on social and general metaphysics rather than on historiography. The historian need not behave differently toward his profession if the thesis is maintained; history must still be written. The problem centers around what is done with history, around interpretations of the historical dimension by non-historians who cannot help making constant use of some conception of the contents of time. It is an issue in resultant attitudes and in the climate of general opinion.

The consequence for liberal religious thought would be that its connections with its antecedents remain effective, that some part of what it is can be said to be what it once was, and that such a judgment is not merely upon its past or historic derivations but is also upon its present nature. With Unitarianism the references are to its roots in Congregationalism, Puritanism, and traditional Catholic Christianity. With Universalism or other movements the principle would refer to various historic lines. If this much is so, then the continuity of religious ideas should be confirmable through cross-sectional or horizontal studies of thought patterns common to diverse systems which are closely related in time. This we have elsewhere remarked to be so.

At this juncture someone is sure to observe that the twentieth century clearly does not look like the twelfth, and aren't we being a little silly? The point may be that different periods attend to different sets of questions or insights. It is as if it were a social duty for them to do so, to enable the exploration and definition of new ranges of possibility. The penalty involved is that the enormous areas of common inheritance become recessive or are overlooked, and are not likely to be brought to notice again unless the earlier questions are also raised anew, perhaps in a new form. The suspicion may be that if a set of questions peculiar to one age were raised again in another age, even in a revised and appropriate form, it would be difficult to answer them even in the revised order of discourse without coming very close to the assumptions contained in the original questions. Apparently, therefore, the metaphysics of liberalism and the metaphysics of traditionalism, general and social, would tend to make similar assumptions and in the end to describe the nature and condition of man in similar terms.

It may then be cause for concern whether the habit of liberal opposition to the traditional ought to be maintained as it now exists—indeed whether contemporary society can afford the luxury of maintaining it. Conversely, it may also be cause for concern whether traditional Catholic Christianity can permit itself the luxury of excluding from its larger pattern the painful dissents of its spiritual children.

This is not to say that religious liberals should forthwith become traditional Christians, or that traditional Christianity should immediately rack itself to encompass a diversity of indigestible sub-viewpoints. Rather it is to suggest that both liberal and traditional groups realize that they are parts of an extended and enduring relation, and that both undertake to see how a generalized conception of the nature of ideological expression operates to justify alike the streams of tradition and dissent, eventually subsuming both in a larger traditional pattern.

Numerous reservations can be entered concerning the sociologies of recent times, but one thing they may have taught us is the substance of the group dimension as one aspect of the real. The fundamental dimension of individual salvation with which in some measure all religious groups are concerned may now have had added unto it the idea already noted of the group or movement as a large-scale experiment to discover and develop new facets of possibility and of reality. That this is so in the social realm may be only an extension of individual insight in tradition and dissent which has always served the purpose. The central notion in both dimensions is the continuing articulation of life and idea.

It is difficult to essay a new approach to an old problem in a brief compass without running the gauntlet of rooted prejudgments of many kinds and ages. Perhaps no religious problem is more difficult than that of the tumbled strands of Christendom. To make a beginning at understanding its complexities may require first an understanding of the nature of one's own tradition at least over the range of its particular existence. For any who may be interested to pursue the liberal tradition the studies by Earl Morse Wilbur, Conrad Wright, Ernest Cassara, and David B. Parke have provided an indispensable base for understanding in the vertical dimensions of Unitarian and Universalist thought. The current period is also producing strong new histories of Protestantism and Catholicism, sometimes by Protestants and Catholics respectively, but increasingly, scholarly accounts of one major tradition by writers from another tradition. Of immense interest on all sides is the rising frequency of useful works speaking across religious lines.

If the radically new conditions of the space age call for a departure from the old luxuries of the separate histories and traditions it may be high time for the liberal church to re-assess the dubious values of its recurrent attack on traditional Catholic Christianity. This is a most complicated social and theological issue and there are other sides to the coin. At the moment one can do no more—but also no less—than to raise the question as one which may immediately require careful rethinking.

So many times a simple fancy comes to mind along with an issue of complex and difficultly abstract nature. In the present instance Longfellow's lightsome verses, "The Arrow and the Song," returning from a childhood of long ago, insistently echo along with the thought:

> "I shot an arrow into the air,
> It fell to earth, I knew not where . . ."

It is as if a movement among ideas by reason of its nature were to take off on its own course, projecting itself into the future independently of tradition till it appeared to have its own substantiality and its own reason for existence, achieving its own description of the real, no longer aware that the multi-dimensional nature of reality requires a complexity of descriptions, certain that its own version is final and free of error, accounting for all allowable phenomena.

> "I breathed a song into the air,
> It fell to earth, I knew not where . . . "

But every flight of fancy, every leap of imagination, every formulation of knowledge, must return at last to the medium of its origin, if not to its precise point of departure, certainly to level of awareness from which it sprang. Here it must find its meanings for human life. Man may reach, but he does not encompass. Life is of the order of reaching; it is not of the order of grasping. Knowledge, we have supposed, is different, definite, in touch with the irreducible. But knowledge, too, and physical reality itself, are constructs, flights of fancy if we like, perhaps among the noblest leaps of mind—but constructs still. Strands of history and movements of thought are no more than parts of this construction. The arrow may be found again in an oak, the song in the heart of a friend. The point is, that which flies must return to earth in the end. It is not permitted to forget its arching pathway in the skies. Not the briefest span of religious dissent can be understood in its fullness except in this way, as a living part of an enduring whole which constantly gives it life and to which in turn it constantly contributes life. Nor can the Catholic Christian tradition of the West understand itself or be understood by others except as efficient source of religious life and energy used to such diverse ends by its dissenting arms, and then as beneficiary of some of the values of dissent. Religion, too, is one.

XIV Return from Enlightenment

For more than the two hundred years which have passed since the Enlightenment considerable segments of Western civilization have been sitting around waiting for the universe to drop the other shoe. This is to say, where the search for knowledge has been a central concern the source of certainty as to the nature of things has increasingly become the natural world, objective as it was supposed to be. Ways of knowing have come about and habits of dependence have arisen which combine to emphasize the impingement of sensory stimuli on human life as primary description of existence. In primitive empiricism and in early stages of naive objectivism western cultures have stumbled into momentary havens of safety in the midst of exploding unknowns.

Most residents of mid-20th century were brought up in an 18th-century world in which a fact was a fact. Indeed, most individuals living in the West today still hold an 18th-century view of nature and of man's relation to it. It has been a reasonable world. There have been a lot of facts to define and in general westerners have been busy and contented with the work of defining as many of them as possible. How admirable is the nature of man! In his devotion to meaningless drudgery he gives of himself far, far beyond what could fairly be expected of him.

The heritage of the Enlightenment, passed slowly down from the cirro-stratum of the mind to the noisy markets of ideas where men move casually in and out buying suits, exchanging little bits of news, and sipping sodas through colored straws, originally meant to the Western tradition the application of rationality to problems of life and the settings of life. It is not so easy now to remember how the observation of "brute fact," in Whitehead's phrase, came to be associated with scientific thought, enabling a subtle and pervasive fault in common conceptions of science. Simple factism could have been at most the condition of an instant the brief course of which flashed past long before the beginning of the 18th century, a sort of May-fly of the mind soon lost in the instantaneous development of rationality indispensable to understanding.

In itself this was quite all right. There has to be rationality for the development of understanding. The oddity is rather that the curious notion of the reliability of facticity, perhaps entailing an active misinterpretation of the nature of a fact, grew to be something of a monster in the scientific tradition. The observation of "brute fact," logically no more than a "point-instant" in the history of thought, was extrapolated in subsequent periods so that the grasp of western science as simply another field in the general realm of rationality, with all that that implies, was often missed. Rationality may have been supposed to be the same as factism, surely error enough if that were all; more than likely, however, the error of "misplaced concreteness" was a by-product of increasing immersion of man in nature and of the description of life as part of nature. Occam's razor cut too deep.

The sense of safety found in scientific studies may have derived from just this error. The Enlightenment was right in ascribing the characteristic of rationality to knowing. Science is today even more a huge structure of rationalistic interconnectedness immediately and intensively dependent on its rationalist components. All systematic knowing is of the order of rationality, unless one chooses to except intuitive and closely related types. The awkwardness between religion and science has been accentuated in the suppositions that perception of nubbly fact was the hallmark of scientific knowledge, that there were generic differences between scientific knowing on one hand and religious, artistic, or historical knowing on the other. These notions were in error.

Facts were indeed the trouble. Even the redoubtable William James assumed that a fact was a fact, and it was useful to do so in his time. But it was not really so. At least to say that it was so did not mean very much for very long unless the operational frame of reference was added into the definition of the fact. As has been noted elsewhere in these pages, operational definition of knowledge conceived broadly over a wide disparity of fields has always been a characteristic of knowing in Western cultures. It was just that the operations had been common to all knowers and to all instances of knowing, and were in effect taken for granted, cancelled out, and ignored. Operational characteristics of knowing were differentiated only when new dimensions of the real were disclosed, so that the setting and operations of an act of knowing had to be detailed. Operational awareness arrived at earlier might well have diverted the

West from the error of misplaced concreteness; operations might have been defined with sufficient breadth and with less metaphysical exclusiveness than later became the case.

Eventually, of course, "facts" disappeared into process and rationality or became relative to situations. Notice that it took the most "modern" of scientific methodologies to bring off a change in the perspective in which science was to be held. It took sophisticated science to replace naive science, and the result, once it had lent itself to careful study from all directions, was clearly no "science" at all in the older sense. One is reminded of the days of the pirates when the best way to scuttle a ship was to point one of its own Long Toms down the hatch and let off a 24-pound shot through the bottom. Then it was reasonably certain the situation would change. Perhaps the new views of science could only have come about in their highly promising forms through scientific operations of the present day.

The scientific tradition is then returning from the mood of the Enlightenment in the sense that the later interpretations of it have tended to support the bifurcation of nature, to separate life from the settings of life, to suggest that knowledge consists of glaring at the hard bones of things. This is not to say that scientific endeavor in itself will be constricted or altered or that it should go back from what it has done. The point is simply that science is a phase of common activity directed toward the study of nature, in which the universal characteristics of knowing are expressed as required by its own operations.

The knowing activity can as well be directed toward the study of human nature, the creation of beauty in art, or the thought of God. It has been sufficiently noted that knowledge is a consequence of a constant relation of subject and object, a relation constructional in quality, supportive of the substance known, partaking of creation by the knower as well as of discovery of objective reality. The real is then a continuum proceeding outward from the self to encompass the full ranges of the universe being known; truth consists of the reliability of the relation tested in individual and group experience. Confirmation of an objective datum by experimental check is just one type of assurance, singled out for special weighting in recent centuries by the cultural accident of abrupt expansions of scientific disciplines.

Error can inhere in any phase of the knowing relation. Distortion is possible on the subjective end. An operational instrument can be at fault, as in red-green colorblindness in a human instrument, or mechanico-electronic error in other kinds of instruments. Finally, a substantive error might occur on the objective end, for facticity must continue to be sharply under study. Factness is no longer referred to with any certainty of what a fact is.

The resolution of intellective dichotomy being considered here takes its departure from a view of the conceptual nature of knowing, which in turn is generalized from simple behaviorisms untrammelled by philosophic consequence into the sphere of humanoid operations; functions of the physical and conceptual self are conceived of as instrumental. On these instruments of selection from chaos or possibility particular realities depend.

The bents of modern times require that scientific thought be put in perspective even while the very brilliance of its achievements have left it running free in many realms. If it is true as we have thought to say, that science has pervaded the reflective fields on the basis of its supposed articulation with the natural universe, then an enormous error has been committed. The sciences can arch a cantilever over the abyss, even build a useful structure on it and use the structure. But they cannot tell the relentless mind of man what it demands to know—what is the nature of the real?

Western civilization should move now from an age of science, conceived of as a methodology for factual discovery and compilation, into an age of common thought. In this the dimensions of awareness apply to all modes of existence. In this sense, of course, religion is a field of awareness; where science has often been regarded as the principal source of knowledge and religion as a region of valuative, moral, or emotional concern, the larger perspective suggests that science is rather a phase of the total religious dimension of existence.

Is there then a pragmatic difference between "science" and "religion"? Between them ranges the common philosophy of awareness in response to the human demand for all possible relation with extensions of the real. Religion is in addition the philosophy of meaning and relation which includes the relation of awareness, in the deepest and widest sense. Science is again what it has actually always been, the philosophy of nature, long recognized as such in the perspective of Thomistic thought, in the Protestant centuries standing apart from its grounds, its clothing and community forgotten, starkly in the midst of things, greatly trying for wholeness where wholeness could not be. The cultural service of the scientific tradition is enormous and will continue to enlarge. It is simply required now that the world-view of the West should see the scientific tradition in a general frame of reference. That there are consequences for religion as for science will be clear enough; a task remaining is certainly that of working out the religious implications of conceptual knowing and of an age of common thought.

It is left to say again, if it should not already be clear, that the degree of motion among positions noted in these papers is really very slight, a motion among centers of gravity in the realm of ideas, as in fact motions among ideas most often are. As the ranges of data to be covered in the several positions are in large part identical ranges by virtue of the human demand for coherence and familiarity the degree of motion could not be large. It is merely that slightest of motions which yet makes all the difference. No major alteration in the configuration of modern thought is contemplated or implied. The scientist will not work differently if the present view should be accepted than he would if it were declined. Cultural specialization would require him to continue in his methodology for the greatest achievements in particular disciplines. The question is rather, what will be the effects in the longest possible view of an altered perspective of scientific endeavor?

Some part of the difficulty of thinking clearly in an analytic age is that the age is quite literally not acquainted with its own general ideas. It is ignorant of its comprehensive assumptions. This is not as odd as it sounds; many cultural periods have surely not known in any conscious way what their general assumptions were. But where the order of generality is at stake an age dominated by analysis is necessarily more ignorant than other periods. If the significance of generality is denied, as the positivists and analysts do, making a prior metaphysical judgment against the ideal order, then the reflective work of the time is simplified and compassable. A fully analytic age would not know anything of meaningful dimensions. Fortunately it is difficult to obtain unanimity in philosophic matter; invariably there is sufficient disagreement to ensure the doing of the world's work.

Curiously enough, science itself is a highly rational and rationalistic set of disciplines, just as it ought to be and just as the Enlightenment thought it was. Neither the 18th nor the 20th century has been in error on this point. Greater errors have been made about science than have been made by science, some of them however by scientists as well as by non-scientists, for scientists are human and make all the errors men normally make, just as religious people do. And this, too, is not to be wondered at; certainly many of the errors made about religion, about secularism, about art history, have been made by religious persons, secularists, or art historians.

The error made over science was the error of a general assumption, the error of "misplaced concreteness," of the supposed facticity of its objects of study. It has been a pervasive error, grasping, elbowing, manipulative, so rude that it has all but shouldered out more careful forms of thought. One can but have one's fling at it.

Observe the crippling consequence for individual life of the conviction that reality lies exclusively outside the self. Passivity descends; originality declines; life's glory fades, and passes into grey. A man waits quietly for the universe to tell him what to do, moving only to satisfy thin needs. He does not come to know himself in depth and breadth; he is ignorant of his stupendous reach and grasp, his piercing insight. He is content to live with lesserness; he thinks less, feels less, does less, creates less, understands less. He may drink more alcohol and use more drugs, striving to find what he fails to realize he has always had. If a man is willing to become the creature of the natural universe he denies his uniqueness and originality, sits leadenly, waiting for the myriad of other shoes to fall.

There is grave risk that science misunderstood, science overweighted, will inadvertently have done just such execution upon the human spirit, for among the profoundest insights of religion remains the principle that a man's life is realized when it is "lost," submerged in awareness of transcendence, in Divinity. Then by a strange and enduring contradiction man is free, free to range the universe he has transcended. This is the meaning of that slightest of motions which yet makes all the difference.

Bibliographic Notes

Allen, J. W., *English Political Thought, 1603-1660.* London, 1938.
Allport, Gordon W., *The Individual and His Religion.* N. Y., 1950.
Auer, J. A. C. Fagginger, *Humanism States Its Case.* Boston, 1933.
Ayer, A. J., *Language, Truth and Logic.* N. Y., 1936.
——, *The Problem of Knowledge.* Baltimore, 1956.
——, *The Foundations of Empirical Knowledge.* London, 1961.

Barber, Bernard, *Science and the Social Order.* Glencoe, 1952; N. Y., 1962.
Barton, Allen, *Studying the Effects of College Education.* New Haven, 1959.
Bateson, Gregory, and Margaret Mead, "Principles of Morale Building." *J. Educ. Sociology,* 1941, *15,* 206-220.
Bergson, Henri, *Creative Evolution.* N. Y., (1911) 1944.
Bixler, Julius Seelye, *Religion in the Philosophy of William James.* Boston, 1926.
——, *Religion for Free Minds.* N. Y., 1939.
——, *Conversations With An Unrepentant Liberal.* New Haven, 1946.
Blanchard, Alberton Maurice, "Music and Memories." North Montpelier, Vermont, *Driftwind, 8,* 3, 73-76 (Sept. 1933). (Courtesy Vt. Hist. Society.)
Bliss, Sylvia H., "The Origin of Laughter." *American J. of Psychology,* XXVI, Apr. 1915.
——, *Quests.* Montpelier, Vermont, 1920, 1965.
——, *Sea Level.* North Montpelier, Vt., 1933.
Bliss, William R., "Role of the Resonance Theory." *The Military Chaplain,* 1950, XX, 3, 17-18.
Bober, Mandell M., *Karl Marx's Interpretation of History.* Cambridge, Mass. 1948.
Bridgman, Percy W., *The Nature of Physical Theory.* Princeton, 1936.
——, *The Logic of Modern Physics.* N. Y., 1927, 1948.
——, *The Way Things Are.* Cambridge, Mass. 1959.
Brinton, Crane, *A Decade of Revolution.* N. Y., 1934.
——, *The Anatomy of Revolution.* N. Y., 1938, 1952.
Broad, C. D., *Scientific Thought.* London, 1927, 1952.
——, *The Mind and Its Place in Nature.* London, 1929. (Courtesy of Robert Mattuck.)
——, *Five Types of Ethical Theory.* London, 1934.
Buber, Martin, *I and Thou.* N. Y., 1937, 1958.
——, *Between Man and Man.* Boston, 1947, 1955.
——, *Eclipse of God.* N. Y., 1952, 1957.
——, *Hasidism and Modern Man.* N. Y., 1958.
——, *Two Types of Faith.* N. Y., 1961.
Bugbee, Henry G., *The Inward Morning.* N. Y., 1961.
Burtt, Edwin A., *Metaphysical Foundations of Modern (Physical) Science.* London, 1924, 1949.
——, *Types of Religious Philosophy.* N. Y., 1951.

Cadbury, Henry Joel, *The Making of Luke-Acts.* N. Y., 1927.
——, *The Peril of Modernizing Jesus.* N. Y., 1937.
——, *Jesus: What Manner of Man.* N. Y., 1947.
Cassara, Ernest, *Hosea Ballou, The Challenge to Orthodoxy.* Boston, 1961.
Cassirer, Ernst, *The Myth of the State.* New Haven, 1946, N. Y., 1955.
——, *The Problem of Knowledge.* New Haven, 1950.
——, *Philosophy of the Enlightenment.* Boston, 1955.
Chan, Wing-tsit, *Religious Trends in Modern China.* N. Y., 1953.
——, *A Source Book in Chinese Philosophy.* Princeton, 1963.
China Mainland Press and Magazine Surveys, issued by the U. S. Consul-General, Hong Kong, on deposit in selected university libraries. (Courtesy of the University of Vermont.)
Churchill, Winston, *The Unknown War: The Eastern Front.* N. Y., 1932.
——, *The Second World War.* I-IV. Boston, 1949-1953.
Collingwood, R. G., *The Principles of Art.* Oxford, 1938, 1961.
——, *The Idea of Nature.* Oxford, 1945.
——, *The Idea of History.* Oxford, 1948.
Conant, James Bryant, *On Understanding Science.* New Haven, 1947.
——, Cambridge Platform Address, 1949.
——, *Science and Common Sense.* New Haven, 1951.
——, *Modern Science and Modern Man.* N. Y., 1952.
——, *Harvard Case Histories in Experimental Science.* Cambridge, Mass., 1957.
——, *Two Modes of Thought.* N. Y., 1964.
Coulson, C. A., *Science and Christian Belief.* Chapel Hill, 1955.
Creel, H. G., *Sinism, A Study of the Chinese World View.* Chicago, 1929.
——, *Confucius, The Man and the Myth.* N. Y., 1949.
——, *Chinese Thought from Confucius to Mao Tse-tung.* Chicago, 1953.

Davis, Arthur Kent, "Some Sources of American Hostility to Russia." *American J. of Sociology,* LIII, 174-183. 1947.
——, "Bureaueratic Patterns in the Navy Officer Corps." *Social Forces,* 27, 143-153. Dec. 1948.
——, "Conflict Between Major Social Systems: The Soviet-American Case." *Social Forces,* 30, 29-36. Oct. 1951.
——, "Anti-Communism and Fascism." *Monthly Review,* V, 2. June 1953.
——, "The Present As History: A Review." *Monthly Review,* V, 8. Dec. 1953.
——, "A New Look at Chinese History, Parts I & II." *Monthly Review,* VII, 10 & 11. Febr. & Mar. 1956.
——, "Juvenile Delinquency Under Capitalism and Socialism." *Monthly Review,* VIII, 5. Sept. 1956.
——, "China's Great Road." *Monthly Review,* VIII, 8. Dec. 1956.
——, "Thorstein Veblen Reconsidered." *Science and Society,* 21: 52-85. Winter 1957.
——, "*Thorstein Veblen: The Postwar Essays.*" *Monthly Review,* IX, 3 & 4. July & Aug. 1957.
——, "Deformation of Society." *The Nation,* 186: 588-589. June 28, 1958.
——, "Sociology Without Clothes." *Monthly Review,* XI, 7. Nov. 1959.
——, "Reflections on Alienation." *Monthly Riview,* XI, 10. Febr. 1960.
——, "Decline and Fall." *Monthly Review,* XII, 6. Oct. 1960.

Davis, Harold M., "An Engineer Looks at the Church." Nashua, N. H., privately distributed, 1934.
——, "The Partnership Plan." Boston, Unitarian Laymen's League, ca. 1935 & ff.
Dewey, John, *The Quest for Certainty.* N. Y., 1929.
——, *A Common Faith.* New Haven, 1934, 1944.
——, *Theory of Valuation.* Chicago, 1939, 1955.
——, and Arthur Bentley, *Knowing and the Known.* Boston, 1949.
——, *Reconstruction in Philosophy.* Boston, (1920) 1957.
Durkheim, Emile, *Elementary Forms of the Religious Life.* Glencoe, (1915) 1947.
Eddington, Sir Arthur, *The Philosophy of Physical Science.* N. Y., 1939.
Eiseley, Loren C., *The Immense Journey.* N. Y., 1957.
——, *Darwin's Century.* N. Y., 1958.
——, *The Firmament of Time.* N. Y., 1960.
Eisenhower, Dwight D., *Crusade in Europe.* N. Y., 1948.
Eskelund, Karl, *The Red Mandarins.* London, 1959.

Fenn, William Wallace, *The Theological Method of Jesus.* Boston, 1938.
Fung, Yu-lan, *A Short History of Chinese Philosophy.* N. Y., 1960.

Geiger, George R., *Towards An Objective Ethics.* Yellow Springs, 1938.
——, *Philosophy and the Social Order.* Boston, 1947.
——, *John Dewey in Perspective.* N. Y., 1958.
Giles, H. Harry, *Education and Human Motivation.* N. Y., 1957.
Guerard, Albert, *Napoleon III.* N. Y., 1955.

Hamlin, Wilfrid G., Ed., *Teacher, School, Child.* Plainfield, Vt., Trustees of Goddard College, 1964.
Heim, Karl, *Christian Faith and Natural Science.* N. Y., 1953.
Hewitt, Arthur Wentworth, *Steeples Among the Hills.* Cincinnati, 1926.
——, *Highland Shepherds.* Chicago, 1939.
——, *God's Back Pasture.* Chicago, 1941.
——, *The Shepherdess.* Chicago, 1943.
——, *Jerusalem the Golden.* Nashville, 1944.
——, *The Bridge.* N. Y., 1948.
Hocking, William Ernest, *The Meaning of God in Human Experience.* New Haven, 1912, 1944.
——, *Human Nature and Its Re-Making.* New Haven, 1923.
——, *Present Status of the Philosophy of Law and of Rights.* New Haven, 1926.
——, *Types of Philosophy,* N. Y., 1929.
——, *The Spirit of World Politics.* N. Y., 1932.
——, *The Lasting Elements of Individualism.* New Haven, 1937, 1940.
——, *Living Religions and a World Faith.* N. Y., 1940.
——, *What Man Can Make of Man.* N. Y., 1942.
——, *Science and the Idea of God.* Chapel Hill, 1944.
——, *The Meaning of Immortality in Human Experience.* N. Y., (1937) 1957.
Holmes, John Haynes, *Rethinking Religion.* N. Y., 1938.

Irwin, William A., and J. M. P. Smith, *The Prophets and Their Times.* Chicago, 1941, 1960.
Irwin, William A., *The Problem of Ezekiel. Chicago, 1943.*

Jacob, Philip, *Changing Values in College.* N. Y., 1957.
James, William, *The Will to Believe.* N. Y., 1896, 1956.
——, *The Varieties of Religious Experience.* N. Y., 1902, 1929.
——, *Pragmatism.* N. Y., 1907, 1931.
——, *A Pluralistic Universe.* N. Y., 1909, 1920.
——, *Essays in Radical Empiricism.* N. Y., 1912, 1922.
——, *Selected Papers on Philosophy.* N. Y., 1917-18, 1929.
——, *Some Problems of Philosophy.* N. Y., 1911.

Kent, Louise Andrews, *Mrs. Appleyard's Year.* N. Y., 1944.
——, and Elizabeth Kent Gay, *The Summer Kitchen.* Boston, 1957.
——, and Elizabeth Kent Gay, *The Winter Kitchen.* Boston, 1962, 1963.
Kierkegaard, Soren, *Purity of Heart Is To Will One Thing.* N. Y., 1939, 1948.
——, *The Point of View For My Work As An Author.* N. Y., 1939, 1962.
——, *Fear and Trembling; The Sickness Unto Death.* N. Y., (1941 . . .), 1955.
——, *The Concept of Dread.* Princeton, 1944.
——, *Concluding Unscientific Postscript.* Princeton, 1944, 1953.
——, *The Attack Upon Christendom.* Princeton, 1944; Boston, 1956.
Kubie, Lawrence, *The Neurotic Distortion of the Creative Process.* Lawrence, Kansas, 1958.
——, "Pavlov, Freud, and Soviet Psychology." *Monthly Review,* IX, 11. March, 1958.

Leonard, William Ellery, *The Locomotive God.* New York, 1927.
Levenson, Joseph R., *Confucian China and Its Modern Fate.* Berkeley, 1958.
——, *Liang Ch'i-ch'ao and the Mind of Modern China.* Cambridge, Mass., 1959.
——, *China: An Interpretive History from the Beginning to the Fall of Han.* Berkeley, 1969.
Lovejoy, Arthur O., *The Great Chain of Being.* Cambridge, Mass., 1933, 1936.
——, *Essays in the History of Ideas.* Baltimore, 1948.

Malalasekera, G. P., *Encyclopedia of Buddhism.* London, 1961-64.
Maritain, Jacques, *Existence and the Existent.* N. Y., 1948, 1957.
——, *Man and the State.* Chicago, 1951, 1962.
——, *The Range of Reason.* N. Y., 1952.
Mattuck, Israel I., *The Thought of the Prophets.* London, 1953.
——, *Jewish Ethics.* London, 1953.
Merton, Thomas, *The Seven Storey Mountain.* N. Y., 1948.
——, *The Waters of Siloe.* N. Y., 1949.
——, *The Sign of Jonas.* N. Y., 1953.
Miller, Perry, and Thomas H. Johnson, *The Puritans.* N. Y., 1938.
Murray, John Courtney, *We Hold These Truths.* N. Y., 1960.
——, *The Problem of God.* New Haven, 1964.

Needham, Joseph, *Science and Civilization in China.* I-IV. Cambridge, 1954-62.
——, Science, *Religion and Reality.* N. Y., 1955.
Niebuhr, Reinhold, *Moral Man and Immoral Society.* N. Y., 1932.
——, *An Interpretation of Christian Ethics.* N. Y., 1935.
——, *The Nature and Destiny of Man.* N. Y., 1941-43.

——, *Faith and History.* N. Y., 1949.
——, *The Irony of American History.* N. Y., 1952.

Ong, Walter J., *Ramus, Method, and The Decay of Dialogue.* Cambridge, Mass., 1958.

Parke, David B., *The Epic of Unitarianism.* Boston, 1957.
Partch, Virgil, *It's Hot in Here.* N. Y., 1944.
——, *Water on the Brain.* N. Y., 1945.
Peaston, A. Elliott, *The Prayer Book Reform Movement in the XVIIIth Century.* Oxford, 1940.
——, *Prayer Book Revisions of the Victorian Evangelicals.* London, 1943.
Peirce, Charles Sanders, *Collected Papers. VI.* Cambridge, Mass., 1935.
Pepper, Stephen C., *World Hypotheses.* Berkeley, 1942.
Pfeiffer, Robert H., *Introduction to the Old Testament.* N. Y., 1941.
——, *History of New Testament Times.* N. Y., 1949.

Radhakrishnan, Sir Sarvepalli, *Religion and Society.* London, 1947, 1956.
——, *The Hindu View of Life.* London, 1927, 1954.
Raven, Charles E., *Natural Religion and Christian Theology.* I — *Science and Religion.* II — *Experience and Interpretation.* Cambridge, 1953.
Riencourt, Amaury de, *The Soul of China.* N. Y., 1958.
Royce, Josiah, *The Hope of the Great Community.* N. Y., 1916.
——, *The Philosophy of Loyalty.* N. Y., 1924.
Russell, Bertrand, *Problems of Philosophy.* London, 1912.
——, *Mysticism and Logic.* N. Y., (1917) 1957.
——, *The Scientific Outlook.* N. Y., 1931.
——, *Human Knowledge.* N. Y., 1948.

Sartre, Jean Paul, *Being and Nothingness.* N. Y., 1956.
Schweitzer, Albert, *The Mystery of the Kingdom of God.* London, 1925.
——, *Out of My Life and Thought.* N. Y., 1933.
——, *Indian Thought and Its Development.* N. Y., 1936.
——, *The Philosophy of Civilization. I & II.* London, 1946, 1947.
——, *The Quest of the Historical Jesus.* N. Y., 1948.
——, *Paul and His Interpreters.* London, 1948.
Simpson, George Gaylord, *The Meaning of Evolution.* New Haven, 1949.
Smith, John E., *Royce's Social Infinite.* N. Y., 1950.
——, *The Spirit of American Philosophy.* N. Y., 1963.
Smuts, Jan Christian, *Holism and Evolution.* N. Y., 1926, 1961.
Sperry, Willard Llearoyd, *Reality in Worship.* N. Y., 1925, 1947.
——, *What You Owe Your Child.* N. Y., 1935.
——, *We Prophesy in Part.* N. Y., 1938.
——, *What We Mean By Religion.* N. Y., 1940.
——, *Those of the Way.* N. Y., 1945.
——, *Religion in America.* N. Y., 1945.
Stevenson, Charles, *Ethics and Language.* New Haven, 1944.
Stiernotte, Alfred P. N., *God and Space-Time.* N. Y., 1954.
——, *Mysticism and the Modern Mind.* N. Y., 1959.

Tagore, Rabindranath, *The Religion of Man.* Boston, 1961.
Tillich, Paul, *The Religious Situation.* N. Y., 1932, 1956.
——, *The Protestant Era.* Chicago, 1948.
——, *The New Being.* N. Y., 1955.
——, *Biblical Religion and the Search for Ultimate Reality.* Chicago, 1955.
Tillyard, Eustace M. W., *The Elizabethan World Picture.* London, 1943, 1958.

Whittaker, Sir Edmund, *Space and Spirit.* Chicago, 1948.
Whitehead, Alfred North, *Science and the Modern World.* N. Y., 1925, 1935. (The quotation in II herein is by permission of Macmillan Company, publishers, and is from p. 15 of the 1925 edition.)
Wilbur, Earl Morse, *A History of Unitarianism. I & II.* Cambridge, Mass., 1947, 1952.
Wild, John, *Introduction to Realistic Philosophy.* N. Y., 1948.
——, *Plato's Theory of Man.* Cambridge, Mass., 1948.
——, *Plato's Modern Enemies and the Theory of Natural Law.* Chicago, 1953.
——, *The Challenge of Existentialism.* Bloomington, 1955.
Wright, Charles Conrad, *The Beginnings of Unitarianism.* Boston, 1955.

Index

Abraham, in SK, 26
Absolute, in SK, 29, 127 & ff.; in Marx, 98
Abstractions: 70, 73; and synthesis, 78; universals, 119
Allen, J. W., on the Puritans, 93
America: cf. Colonial, 61 & ff.; intellectual, 67; Puritan and later, 72 & ff.; Soviet-American stand-off, 74, comparison, 75 & ff.
Amos of Tekoa: philosophy of history, 94
Analysis: fun with, 7-8; physical, 17; existential self—, 39; supplemented by cultural wholes, 68; limited tool, 68, 69; relapses into, 70; and meaning, 143
Anselm, St.: ontological argument, in Auer, 132
Antaeus, 100
Antinomianism: difficulties, 71; student instances of, 117
Antioch Review, v
Aquinas, cf. Thomism: 18; as systematic landmark, 21, 26, 31; Thomism, 33, 40, 124; Ultimate in, 123 & ff.; Summa, 123 & ff.; on God, 125-6
Aristotelian: shift from Platonism, 18; realism, 38; Thomism, 124
Army, "New Model": (cf. Williams, George H.), as a church, 97
"Arrow and the Song, The": 137 (Longfellow, H. W.)
Assertive: knowing as, 17, 83, 120; mind as, 17,
Attack Upon Christendom (SK), 24 & ff.; 128
Auer, J. A. C. Fagginger, 66; on Catholicism and "concern", 100; on Chinese Communist lack of humor, 112; as humanist, 129, 131 & ff.; *Humanism States Its Case*, 131; system, idea of God, 131

Augustine, St., 127
Ayer, A. J., 121; 145

Bacon, Roger, 125
Bampton Lectures (James B. Conant, 1952): 8, 53
Barnes, Doris S., vi
Bartlett, Katharine Kendall, viii
Barton, 85
Bateson, G., & Mead, M., 87 & ff.; (cf. Resonance)
Baxter, G. P., vii
Beat, Beatnik: 2; cults, 10
Belief: and force, 64 (cf. Conant, Cambridge Platform Address, 1949); in religion, 90
Bible: and Christianity, 92
Bixler, J. Seelye, vii, 121, 145
Black Arts, student interest in, 118
Bliss, Sylvia H.: *Quests, Sea Level*, 129; as humanist, 129; 145
Bliss, William R., 145
Bober, Mandell M.: on Marxist absolutism, 98
Bridgman, P. W., 3-5; 82; (cf. Operational Thought); 145
Brinton, Crane: patterns of revolution, 75, 76; 96; 145
Buber, Martin, 121; 145
Buddhism, Theravada: as modern, 118; on human nature, 119; view of the natural world, 121; and Christianity (ecumenism), 122-3; ultimate in, 123; vigor of, 129; on speculative questions, 131
Burma, 122
Burtt, E. A., 18, 23; 145
Butler, Anna P., vi

Cadbury, Henry J., vii, 146
Calais, Vermont, viii, 129
Calvinism: and Communism, 91, 97
Cambridge High and Latin School (Mass.), vii

Cassara, Ernest, 136; 146
Catholicism: and Communism, 91 & ff.; force in, 95 & ff.; varieties of, 97; relative sophistication, 60, 93, 99; and Protestantism (ecumenism), 123; as liberal root, 135
Chan, Wing-tsit: on Confucianism, 104
Changing Values in College (Philip Jacob), 79 & ff.
Chickering, Arthur W., viii
China, Mainland: Chinese and Soviet thought, 99; religious themes in, 101 & ff.; *China Press and Magazine Surveys,* 105 & ff.
Choice: SK's view of, 25; grounds of, in ethics, 79
Christianity: in SK, 25, 28, 30; in a university setting, 50 & ff.; renewed emphasis on, in higher education, 52; and Marxism, 53; views of reality, 54; Eastern Orthodox, 76; and ethical tradition, 80; and Communism similar, 90; common inconsistency regarding human capability, 91-2; interim ethic in Marxism and, 94; other-worldliness in Communism and, 94; Kierkegaard and, 126 & ff.; as liberal root, 135, 137
Church: in SK, 24 & ff.; 30, 128; and university, 50 & ff.; and state, separation of, 61; elect in communism and, 92; and communism, 96 & ff.; New Model Army as, 97; Mainland Chinese Communist similarities to, 111
Churchill, Winston, 34; Fulton address, 74
Civilization: as adventure in understanding, 55, 58; as idea and action effort, 101; gigantic guesswork, 63
Coffee, Helen, (Nashua, N. H. Senior High), 131
Colonial America: and religious choice, 64 & ff.; toleration in, as pragmatic, 97 (cf. W. L. Sperry, *Religion in America*)
Commandism: defined, 114-5

Common thought, age of: 53; 142 & ff.
Commonalities: in education, 41 & ff.; constants among cultural periods, 51
Communications: consequences of accelerated, 67
Communism: as religion, 90 & ff., 101; economic environment as Godfool, 91; eschatological nature of, 94; requirement of power, 98; Mainland Chinese, 101 & ff.; church comparison, 111
Community: beloved, 52 (cf. Royce, J., and Sperry, W. L.); small community and religious issues, 64; in conflict with the rebel, 71-2
Conant, James B., 8, 53-4; use of force in history, 64 (Cambridge Platform Address, 1949); 146
Concept of Dread, 128 (SK)
Concept(s), Approach to Philosophy of Conceptualism: operationalist mode, 2-7; 10; past vs. contemporary, 11; as element in definition of the real, 12; constructional, 18; changes as slight, 20; as determinative, 21; as philosophy of knowledge, 23, 86; knowing as conceptual, fundamental, 36-37, 120, 132-3, 142; in progressive education, 44; evanescent, 54; futuristic implications of, 55; of man in education, 58; pace of change heightened, 68; larger fields of reference, 70; partial knowledge through, 82
Concluding Unscientific Postscript, 126 (SK)
Conflict: philosophy of, ix-x; of science and religion, 17 & ff.; and resolution in education, 46; pleasures of, in education, 49; Soviet-American, a family quarrel, 74; absurdity of, 78; oppositions and similarities, 90-91
Confucian thought: themes in, 101 & ff.; Joseph Needham on, 102 & ff.; Wing-tsit Chan, 104; de Riencourt, Creel, Levenson, 104; and Communism, 104; in Mainland Chinese Communism, 116

152

Congregationalism, 135
Constants, 71; cultural, 77
Constructs: constructional thought, 22; existentialism as denial of, 34; in process of change, 56; knowledge as, 69; 81; and education, 85; vs. worldview, 86; outmoded scientific, 89
Contemplation, 21-2, 54, 57
Copernicus, 19
Cornell, Elizabeth F., vi
Cosmology: and philosophy of knowledge, 21; cosmos recreated in progressive education, 44; as projective, 55
Cramer, Martha C., vi
Crane Review, v
Cromwell, Oliver: "New Model" Army, 97 (cf. Williams, George H.)
Crozer Seminary *Quarterly,* v
Culture: motion and thought in, 36 & ff.; existentialism as response to cultural history, 39-40; past as enemy, 43, 45; materials, synthesis of (in progressive education), 44; and education in general, 48; and values, 55; near-identity in, 52, 66 & ff.; differentiation supplemented by wholes, 68; longitudinal and cross-sectional identities, 68-9; essences, 69; defined, 69; constants, 77

Dante, as systematic landmark, 21
Darwin, Charles, 19 & ff., 67, 84
Davis, Harold M.: industrial engineer, on efficiency of God, 130; 147
Deism, pan-: Theravada Buddhism as, 123
Despair, 13; in SK, 29; in perspective, 63
Determinism: as hoopsnake, 89
Dewey, John: as humanist, 130; valuation theory, 130 & ff.; system and metaphysic, 130-131; and Auer, 131-132; 147
Divinity: 13, 26, 31, 35; student as, in progressive education, 44; untouched by relativity in worldviews, 55; in Confucian thought, 102; in Theravada Buddhism, 123; in St. Thomas, 125-6; in SK, 128; realization of life in, 144
Dromore, County Down, viii

Ecumenical issues: 51; in the small community, 64; Buddhist-Christian and Protestant-Catholic, reconceptualizing, 122-3, 135-6; histories across traditional divisions, 136-7
Education: as metaphysical reality, viii; x; and philosophy of knowledge, 23; and method, 23, resonance, 33; as commonality, 41 & ff.; conventional, 41 & ff., 42 & ff.; progressive, 43 & ff., 44 & ff.; what education is, 46, 85; as challenge, 47; force as common element, 47; leadership, 47; views of human nature, 47-8; as metaphysics, 55 & ff., 85; as religion, 60, 63; and values, 79; and moral life, 89; in Mainland China, 109
Educational Theory, v
Ego: Buddhism on the self, 119
Eisenhower, Dwight D.: on force as politics, 97
Eliot, Frederick May, viii
Empiricism: as illusion, 13; evanescent, 17; subsumed by reason, 37; and culture, 38; existential contradiction of, 39; in manufacturing, deficient, 57; expansion of, in classical Buddhism, 120-1; anachronisms in, 134; and 20th century viewpoint, 139
Engels, Friedrich, 91
Enlightenment, 139 & ff.
Epistemology: analytic, vs. conceptualized reality, 21; and reason, 37; of science and religion, 53; in education, 58; Theravada Buddhist, 119-120; systemic place, 121, 132-3; constructionist (conceptualist), 132; as personality projection, 133 (cf. Knowing)

Eskelund, Karl: on Mainland Chinese medicine, 103; *The Red Mandarins,* 115
Ethic; interim, in Communism and Christianity, 95
Ethics: metaphysics and, 13; Confucian, 102
Existentialism(s): as intrusive value, 2; secular, 10, 16, 36; religious, 11, 13, 35; as interstices, 32-40; problem of data in, 35 & ff.; psychologist as, 35-6; as question, 36; subsumed by reason, 37; as cultural reflection, 38; philosophic competence of, 38-9; reason questioned by, 67; and general ideas, 82; Kierkegaard and, 126; epistemology common with other modes of thought, 133; as anachronism, 134
Experience: and subjectivism, 82-3; 121; appeal to, 128

Factism, factness: 139 & ff.; 144 (cf. Knowing, etc.)
Faith: in human nature, selective, 45; mediaeval, in modern science, 53 (A. N. Whitehead); salvation in traditional religion, 92; Communist and Christian, 92-3; and reason in SK, 126; in science, 125
Fascism: relation to prophecy and democracy, 92
Fear and Trembling, 26 (SK)
Fenn, William Wallace, "thought of God", 141; 147
Finite: in SK, 27 & ff.; 127 & ff.
Forbes, George Shannon, vii
Force: as religious characteristic, 64, 97-98 (cf. Violence)
Ford Foundation, vi
Ford, Margaret, vi
Form: and fundament, 77
Fourdrinier, 57
Freud: progressive education and, 46, 48; and Marx, 100
Fung, Yu-lan: philosophical positions of, 108-9

Galileo, 19
Gandhi, Mohandas K., 122
Gay, Elizabeth Kent, viii; 148
Generalities: cf. Ideas, general
Gibran, Kahlil, 129
God: peace in, 12-13; substitutes for, 26; in Puritanism, 72 & ff.; function in secularisms, 73; means of production as, 76; 90-91; kingdom of, and the proletarian state, 92; doctrine of, in Communism and Christianity, 92; Son of, 92; eschatological kingdom, 95; function in thought systems, 118; St. Thomas on, 124 & ff.; as Person and First Principle, 125-6; in Kierkegaard, 126 & ff.; for Dewey, 130 & ff.; and efficiency, 130; Auer and humanism on, 131-2; thought of, 141 (cf. Fenn, W. W.)
Goddard College, Plainfield, Vt., vii, 84
Gravity, philosophic centers of, 15, 16; 51; 52; 143
Guerard, Albert: on Napoleon III, 96

Half-Way Covenant, 72
Hargroves, Thomas, viii
Harvard: iv; Divinity School, 9, 51-2; 130; Memorial Church, 50 & ff.; William James, 56
Hegel: 16; and SK, 27, 126 & ff.; allegedly, on stinking eggs, 116
Hercules, 100
Herriott, Alice Lake, iii
Herriott, Frank W., viii
Historiography, 135
Hocking, William Ernest: vii; 11, 81; 147
Hoitt, Edna P., viii
Holism, 68, (cf. Smuts, J. C.)
Holmes, John Haynes, 32
Humanisms: 129 & ff.; epistemology common with other modes of thought, 132-3
Human nature: conceptions of, 2; role in knowing, 2, 141; as conceptual element in knowing, 2; in general,

12-13; as reflection of Divinity, 13; selective faith in, 45; views of, in educational systems, 47, 48; youth as elect, adult as evil, 47-48; differing reflections in world-views, 55; and philosophy of education, 59; as religious, 65; persistent, 82; as lens, 82, 84; in general, 83-4; controlling knowledge, 83; as spirit, 83; as reservoir, in resonance (q. v.), 87; similar in Communism and Christianity, 91; in liberal thought, 92; systemic question on, 119; Theravada Buddhist, 120 & ff.; as one question in basic triad, 121
Hume: Humeian anachronisms, 134
Humor: lack of, in Chinese Communism, 112; (cf Auer, J.A.C.F.)
Hutchinson, Anne, 71
Huxley, Thomas, 19 & ff.

Idealisms: older and newer, 2, 3-4; Thomist bridge from, 124-5; epistemology common with other modes of thought, 133
Ideas: slightness of movement among, 19-20, 51, 52, 66; 143; general, 20, 56 & ff., 83-84, 143; and judgment (SK), 25 & ff.; as real, conceptual, 37; and learning, 46; event as manifestation of, 56; defined differentially, 66; human nature as key to systems of, 83; relativity of, in Marxism, 98; and time, 134-5; anachronistic, 117-8, 134; (cf. also Gravity, centers of)
Identity, cultural, 53, 66 & ff.
Individualism: unclear in Communism and Christianity, 95; contribution of Protestantism, 123; in SK's religious experience, 128
Infinite: 26, 27 & ff.; 127 & ff.
Influence: philosophic, 32; in ethics, 79 & ff. (cf. Resonance)
Irving, Washington, 63

Jacob, Philip: 79; 84-6
James, William: 56 & ff.; 140; 148

Janus: -relation of definition and discovery, 37
J. of Higher Education, v
Judaism: commentary in, as in Christianity, 93
Judgment, problem of: 7-10; in SK, 27 & ff.

Kantian thought-pattern: Theravada Buddhism as, 123
Keefe, Edmund, vi
Kierkegaard, Soren (SK): 16; 24 &ff.; language problem, 122; non-rationalist experience deriving from, 124; Ultimate in, 118 & ff.; lifestyle, 127; and the Lutheran Church, 128; as operationalist, 128; and Fagginger Auer, 132; 148
Knowing: and reality, x; as art and poetry, 2; as social science, 2-3; as operational, conceptual, common among diverse fields, 8, 36, 39, 53, 86, 120-121, 140-141, 142; mind as central in, 8, 17; self in, 9; philosophy of, 15 & ff.; and motivation, 15; nature of, 15; subjectivity in, 16; kinds of, 16, 141; as one thing, 17; in science and religion, 18, 133, 140 & ff.; as a study, 21 & ff., levels of, 23; kinds of data, 35; education as ways of, 59; evidence in Puritan witness, 72; partial, via concepts, 82; assertive, 83, 86, 120; via revelation, in Communism and Christianity, 94 & ff.; systemic question on, 119; Theravada Buddhism, 120; as relation of subject and object, 122, 132; constructionist (conceptualist), 132, 138, 141; factism and rationality in, 139-140; as creative, 141
Kuanyin, 5
Kubie, Laurence, 86; 148

Law: religious, 93
Lenin: human nature in Communist thought, 91 & ff.

Leonard, William Ellery, 120
Levenson, J. R., 104; 148
Liberalism: human nature in, 13, 89, 92; liberal religion, 134; common metaphysics with traditionalism, 136; histories of Unitarian-Universalism, 136
Lockeian anachronisms, 134
Logic: personal, vii; 35; logical necessity, 124
Longfellow, Henry Wadsworth, 137
Lord, Marion E., vi
Lovejoy, Arthur O., 67

Malalasekera, G. P.: on "point-instants", 121, 140
Man: as conceptualist, 6; as central in nature, 8, 144; Invisible, 14; as spirit, 83-84; common descriptions in liberal and traditional metaphysics, 136; free of bondage to the natural universe, 144
Mao Tse-tung, Chairman: quoted in SCMP, 105; influence on illness, 112-114
Maritain, Jacques, 33; 148
Martensen, H. L., 24, 43, 128
Marxism: as form of Christian thought, 53 (cf. Bober, M. M.); human nature in Christian and Marxist thought, 91; Marx, 93 & ff.; otherworldliness in Christianity and, 94; relativity of ideas, 98; Marx and Freud, 100; Fung Yu-lan on, 108; politics as root (in Chinese Communism), 115
Massachusetts Bay Colony, 61
Materialism: dialectical, as form of traditional Christianity, 92
McArthur, Herbert: vi; "class paradox", 131
Meaning: 10, 12-13, 34; life without general, 52; and personal drama, 54; in education, 58-59; of religion in America, 64; questions of, 78; work of religion as ... Word of God, 92; of life, 137

Metaphysical Foundations of Modern Science (E. A. Burtt), 23
Metaphysics: popular, 22; and psychology, 36; prior metaphysical decision, 37, 40, 143; social reference-points in, 38; in education, 55 & ff., 79 & ff., 88; cultural commonalities, 76, and ethics, 13, 80-1; bridge between ideas and conduct, 86; Confucian social, 162, historical, 109; different in Western and Eastern Communisms, 115; and reason, 123; Dewey's socio-cultural, 130, Auer's humanistic, 131 & ff.; epistemological outreach into, 132; of history, 134 & ff., as historical continuity, 134-5; and religion, 59-60
Michigan, 86
Midwest Quarterly, v
Middle Ages: scientific thought derived from, 53 (cf. Whitehead)
Milinda: King, 117 & ff.
Mind: central in knowing, 8, 12, 17; assertive, 17; creative, 22; in Theravada Buddhism, 120; knowledge as leaps of, 138
Modern Science and Modern Man (1952), 8, 53 (cf Conant)
Moral: choice, 13-14; fundamental dimension, 15; morality and social reference-points, 38; in education, 58, 79 & ff., 88, 89; drift from sources, 64; momentum, 64; dimension of human life, 89; nature of Confucian thought, 104
Morale: "latent", 87 (Bateson and Mead); (cf. also Hocking)
Moriarty, Martha, viii
Motion: among ideas, 19-20, 51, 143, 144
Munn, James B., vii
Murray, John Courtney, 99; 148
Murray, J. Tucker, vii
Mynster, J. P., 24, 28-29, 128
Mysticism: private, a problem to Puritanism, 71 & ff.
Myths: of today and yesterday, 7

Nagasena: on the self, 119 & ff.;
Socratic questioning, 119
Nashua, N. H., vi
Nature: in existential thought, 40;
concepts of, 54; in education, 59;
philosophy of, 59, 142
Needham, Joseph: on Confucian
thought, 102 & ff; 148
Neo-Confucian thought: 104, 116
*Neurotic Distortion of the Creative
Process,* 86 (cf. Kubie, L.)
New England: town meeting, 56; and
Buddhist Burma, 122
"New Model" Army: as a church, 97
(cf. Williams, G. H.)
Newtonian universe, 11
Niebuhr, Reinhold, 121; 148

Objectivity: and freedom, 15; in
education, 59 (cf. subjectivism,
knowing)
Occam, William of : "razor", 140
Oedipus: personalization of relationships, 2
Ofuna, railyards of, 5
Olympus: as functional truth for
Athens, 7
Operational thought: ix; modes of, 3-7;
knowing as, 36, 140 & ff.; from
constructs, 85; SK as religious
operationalist, 128; error in, 141-2;
(cf. Bridgman, P. W.)
Oxbow, in thought, 8

Parke, David B., 136; 149
Partch, Virgil, 43; 149
Particulars: 56 & ff.
Peaston, A. Elliott, viii; 149
Perceptions: mediaeval and modern, 5-6; in depth, 9; possible, 17; casual
data of, 82; and conceptions, 89
Personality: as social relations, 2; onion
theory of, 2; metaphysics of, 3 & ff.;
as element in judgment, 7-10, 11-12;
liberal view of, 13; person as key to
idea systems, 83; Kubie, 86; and
process in Theravada Buddhism, 123
Pfeiffer, Robert H., vii; 149

Phenomenological data: and positivism,
35
Philosophy: in perspective, 15, 71; of
history, 94
Pitkin, Royce S., 84
Platonism: 38; student instances of,
118; Thomist transition to realism,
124; Auer and, 132
"Point-instant", 121, 140
Political forces: as Chinese Communist
metaphysics, 115-116
Positivism: as intrusive value, 2; and
existentialism, 35; "data", as
"existential", 35; and general ideas,
82; student instances of, 118, 134;
epistemology common with other
modes of thought, 133
Process: and personality in Theravada
Buddhism, 123; in epistemological
outreach, 133
Prophetic religion: cf. Religious traits
Protestantism: Calvinistic, and
Catholicism, 91; liberal wing, 92;
discipline in, 96; toleration in, 97;
student instances of, 117; and
Catholicism (ecumenism), 123;
schism terminating, 123; on God,
124; SK as epitome of, 128;
arrogance and humility typical of,
128-9
Psychiatric movement: and existentialism, 34
Psychology: psychologism in existential
thought, 39, 40; Theravada Buddhist
psychology of mind, 119-120; reason
and, in SK, 126; judgment and
feeling in SK, 128; (cf. Religious)
Puritan themes: in 20th century, 71 &
ff.; Allen, J. W., 93; "New Model"
Army, 97; 135

Questions: philosophic, as central, 20;
as philosophy of knowledge, 21;
ultimate, 23; vary with periods, 66;
for wonder, not for answers, 66-7
Quests, 129 (cf. Sylvia H. Bliss)
Quinnipiac College, Hamden, Conn.,
viii

Rationalism: Platonist, 38, 124; less a cultural reflection, 38; in Puritan community, 71, 72; student instances of, 117, 134; common epistemology with humanism, 132-133; Enlightenment, 139; rationality in knowing, 140 & ff. (cf. also Reason)

Real, Reality: 17; 36; realism, 37; emotionally prehended, 39; in American education, 57; in Western and Eastern Communisms, 115-6; Theravada Buddhism on, 119 & ff.; question on the nature of, 118-9; objective realism, 124-5; versions of, 125-6; realistic epistemology common with other modes of thought, 133; in history, 134-5; group dimension of, 136; multidimensional, 137; and the self, 144

Reason: as conceptual instrument, 36-38; existentialist questioning of, 67; as faculty, in St. Thomas, 123 & ff.; as means of comprehending God, 125; and faith, in SK, 126; Enlightenment, 139 & ff.

Reflective thought: 33; 66, 134 (cf. Thought)

Register-Leader, v

Religion: in perspective, 15; as form of knowing, 17 & ff.; 142; and humanistic studies, 53; and scientific studies, 17, 53-4, 133; and Marxism, 53; multiple foci in, 55; in education, 58, 59 & ff.; and metaphysics, 59; in small communities, 64; larger conceptual patterns, 70; and scientific view, 89, 142 & ff.; and Communism, 90, 101; objects vs. forms of belief, 90; prophetic mood, 92; salvation by faith, 92; violence and toleration, 97; Confucian question, 102; liberal, 134 & ff.; enduring antecedents of liberal, 135; liberal histories, 136; as one, 138, 142-3; as transcendence, 144

Religious psychology and traits: prophetic mood, 92, 129; government by elect as a, 92; fanatic self-deception as, 93; otherworldliness in Communism and Christianity, 94; discipline and order, 96; Quaker-type "concern", 96; theme of the Golden Age, 97; force as, 64, 97; absolutism, 98-99; indifference as negative dimension, 100; moral inspiration and institutionalization (Confucian), 104; customs in China, 106 & ff.; Chinese Communist psychology as, 108; conversion, 111; humor (in Chinese Communism), 112; instance of, 112; faith in science, 125; reason and psychology in SK, 126; SK as religious psychologist, 127; arrogance and humility as, 128-9; (cf. Psychology)

Renaissance: and Thomism, 125

Resonance: transmission of ideas and philosophic "influence" as, 33 (cf. W. E. Hocking, Bateson and Mead, W. R. Bliss); 87 & ff.; in Chinese Communism, 111

Revolution: as eschatological, 94-95; and faith in Communism and Christianity, 94

Rochester, Vermont, 129 (cf. Sylvia Bliss)

Royce, Josiah: "beloved community of memory and hope" (adapted by Dean Sperry), 52; 149

Ruggli, Eva M., vi

Russell, Bertrand, 129; 149

Salem witch trials, 72

Salvation: in SK, 31; in progressive education, 45; without grace, as American theme, 72; in Calvinism, 91; in traditional religion, 92-93; group dimension added, 136

Sampson, Ethel V., vi

Sartre, J. P., 36, 121

Schroeder, Adele, vi

Schweitzer, Albert, 81; 149

158

Science and the Modern World (Whitehead): 18; 19; influence of mediaeval thought, 53

Science: social, 1-2; as self-discovery and re-description, 7; of man as purposefully limited, 11; limitations of, 12; as form of knowing, 17 & ff.; and religion, 17 & ff., 53 & ff.; as faith, 18; larger fields of reference, 4, 70; and religion holding common epistemology, 133; defined, 141; from an age of, 142; as philosophy of nature, 142; over-weighted, 144

Scientific: method in flux, 7; method and existentialism, 35, 39; descriptions limited, 83; discourse as subjective, 89; view as religious, 89, 142; faith, 125; thought as "brute fact", 139; factism, 139; return from Enlightenment mode of scientific thought (factism), 141; 142; as rational, 143

Sea Level, 129 (cf. Bliss, Sylvia H.)

Secularism: and existentialism, 10, 34; as illusion, 65; secular first cause as God, 73; Catholicism and, 100

Self: and subjectivism, 9; Hocking on, 11; existentialism and, 35; as conceptual, 36-7, 132; as lens, 37, 82; and learning, 46; Ego in Theravada Buddhism, 119 & ff.; systemic place of, 121; SK's Angst in, 128; in the knowing relation, 141; and reality, 144

Shea, Agnes, viii

SK: cf. Kierkegaard, Soren

Smuts, J. C.: holism, view toward cultural wholes, 68; 149

Sociology: contribution to metaphysics, 136

Socratic: knowledge of the good, 80; questioning in Theravada Buddhism, 119

Soul: 10-13; Hocking on, 11; 17; in SK, 26, 31; 64

Soviet: and other western ideologies, common elements in, 74 & ff.; first cause, 76; Communism and Christianity, 90 & ff.; and Mainland Chinese Communisms, 99

Sperry, Willard Llearoyd, vii, 9, 51; favorite description of Harvard as the "beloved community of memory and hope" (adapted from Royce), 52; religious toleration in America as pragmatic, 97; 149

Spirit: Hegelian, 27; human, 83-84; 85; 144

Spring, Elizabeth, viii

Stalin, Joseph: memorialized in Mainland China, 106

Stevenson, Charles, 121; 149

Stiernotte, Alfred P. N., viii

Subjectivity: subjectivism as intrusive value, 2; as dilemma, 9, in general, 10, existential, 16, and general ideas, 82, and experience, 82; SK and Auer, 132; in knowing, 15-16; subject and object, 123

Summa Theologica, 123

Systems: and the teacher, 46; of education, 47, 59; of abstractions, 66; role in cultural identity, 77; of ideas, 83; and the student, 118, 134; and dialogic questions, 118 & ff.; Kierkegaard on, 126 & ff.; metaphysical outreach in, 132; continuity in, 134-5

Taoism: Needham on, 102-3

Tarwater, Alexander, viii

Teaching, as resonance, 33

Temperament: and worldview, 81 & ff.; 85

Tension: in SK, 29; in higher education, 52

Thomism: 40; 123 & ff.; as modern, 125; and post-mediaeval periods, 125; philosophy of nature, 142 (cf. Aquinas)

Thoreau, H. D., 122

Thought: patterns and behaviors of, ix; systems of, 5, 133; constructs in, 11, 22; morphology of, 38 & ff.; 40; forms responsive to states of knowledge, 67; modes of, 67;

assumptions re-examined, 68; of God, 141 (cf. Fenn, W. W.); age of common, 142 & ff. (cf. Reflective thought)
Tillich, Paul, 121; 150
Tillyard, Eustace M. W., 67
Toynbee, Arnold: philosophy of history, 94
Tradition: 9; third generation phenomenon, 62-3; God-function comparable in Communism, 90-1; Chinese respect for, 105; common metaphysics of traditionalism and liberalism, 136; scientific, 143
Transcendence: religion as, 144
Transcendentalism: student instances of, 117
Truth: in SK, 26, 127-128; in all traditions, 55; defined 141

Ultimate : religious ideas of, 55; reality in Western and Eastern Communisms, 115-116; focal question on, 118 & ff., defined, 121, in Theravada Buddhism, 118-123; in Thomism, 123-125; in SK, 126-129; in humanisms, 129-132
Union Theological Seminary, New York, viii
Unitarian-Universalism: 134 & ff.; root connections operative, 135; histories, 136
United Nations, 122
Universals: questions of, 119-120
U Thant, 122

Value(s): culture as testing of, 55; systems, 63; and college, 79 & ff.; consistent in acentric universe, 84 & ff.; Dewey on, 130 & ff.

Vermont: University of, vi; in 20th century, 67; viii, 129
Violence: in Communism and Christianity, 95 & ff.; relative sophistication, 157

Wallace, Alfred Russel, 84
Way Things Are, The (Bridgman): 82
Wells, H. G., "The Invisible Man", 3
Whitehead, A. N., 18; 38; science derived from mediaeval thought, 53; climate of opinion, 68, 135; student devotees of "brute fact", 118, and scientific thought, 139; fallacy of misplaced concreteness, 141, 144; 150
Wilberforce University (Ohio), vii-viii
Wilbur, Earl Morse, 136; 150
Wild, John, 38; 150
Williams, G. H.: on Cromwell's "New Model" as a church, 97
Wordsworth, "Westminster Bridge", iii
Worldview(s): 6-7; as context, 18; conceptual, 20; existential, 34; varied cultural, 55; as envelope, 62; assumptions rarely reviewed, 66; within the self, 67; differential definitions superannuated, 68; as ground of morality, 79, 80 & ff.; Hocking on, 81; and temperament, 81 & ff.; as enabler of knowledge, 82 & ff.; and education, 84 & ff.; limited, 86; risk of idolatry, 87; metaphysical outreach in, 132; human relations and, 133
Wright, C. Conrad, 136; 150

Yale Review, The, v